Smart Travel Guide to 16 National Parks in the Western United States

Camping & Hiking Guide

(Also In –Depth Guide to Yosemite, Olympic & Grand Canyon)

By

Rob J. Simms

Published by:

CSBA Publishing House

Cover & Interior designed

By

Denise Nicholson

First Edition

TABLE OF CONTENTS

Acknowledgements 7

Introduction 8

Part – 1 9

16 National Parks Of the West 9

Channel Islands, California 10

Death Valley, California 14

Joshua Tree, California 18

Sequoia & Kings, California 22

Lassen Volcanic, California 25

Pinnacles, California 28

Redwood, California 31

Yosemite, California 35

Crater Lake, Oregon 40

Mount Rainier, Washington 44

North Cascades, Washington 48

Olympic, Washington 51

Great Basin, Nevada 56

Saguaro, Arizona 60

Petrified Forest, Arizona 64

Grand Canyon, Arizona 67

Part -2 72

What to See & Do in a Day Trip 72

Channel Islands, California 73

Death Valley, California 76

Joshua Tree, California 78

Sequoia & Kings, California 80

Lassen Volcanic, California 84

Pinnacles, California 87

Redwood, California 89

Yosemite, California 92

Crater Lake, Oregon 94

Mount Rainier, Washington 96

North Cascades, Washington 98

Olympic, Washington 100

Great Basin, Nevada 102

Saguaro, Arizona 104

    West Tucson Mountain District 105

    East Rincon Mountain District 105

Petrified Forest, Arizona 107

    Painted Desert Rim Trail...107

    Puerco Pueblo 108

    Blue Mesa 108

    Crystal Forest 108

    Giant Logs 108

    Long Logs 109

    Agate House 109

Grand Canyon, Arizona 110

  South Rim Day Hikes 110

    Rim Trail...110

    Bright Angel Trail 111

    South Kaibab Trail 111

    Hermit Trail 111

    Grandview Trail 112

  North Rim Day Hikes 112

    Bright Angel Point Trail 112

    Transept Trail..113

    Bridle Trail 113

    North Kaibab Trail 113

    Ken Patrick Trail 114

    Uncle Jim Trail 114

    Widforss Trail 114

    Cape Royal Trail 114

    Cliff Springs Trail 115

    Roosevelt Point Trail 115

Part – 3 ....**116**

14-Day Park Hopper Travel Plans..**116**

2-Week Trip Itineraries 116

Itinerary #1: Southern California 117

  Channel Islands, Joshua Tree, Death Valley, Sequoia & Kings, Yosemite, Pinnacles ..117

    Channel Islands...117

    Death Valley 120

    Easy Hikes 121

    Moderate Hikes 121

    Difficult Hikes 122

    Joshua Tree 123

    Sequoia and Kings 126

Yosemite...128

Pinnacles...130

Itinerary #2: Washington 132

   Mount Rainier, Olympic, North Cascades..132

      Mount Rainier 132

      Olympic National Park 134

      North Cascades 136

      Easy Hikes 137

      Moderate Hikes 138

      Strenuous Hikes 138

Part – 4 ....**140**

A Detail In-Depth Look Inside 3 Most Popular Parks...........................**140**

In-Depth Guide to Yosemite National Park 141

   Yosemite Valley 141

      Visitor Centers and Museums 141

      Activities 142

      Hiking Trails 143

   Points of Interest 143

      Waterfalls 143

      Tunnel View 145

   Wawona and Mariposa Grove 146

      Visitor Centers and Museums 146

      Activities 146

      Hiking Trails 147

   Points of Interest 147

      Chilnualna Falls..147

      Mariposa Grove 147

   Tuolumne Meadows and Tioga Road...147

      Visitor Centers and Museums 148

      Activities 148

      Hiking Trails 149

   Points of Interest 149

   Hetch Hetchy 151

      Activities 151

      Hiking Trails 151

Points of Interest 152
Crane Flat Area 152

    Activities 153
    Hiking Trails 153

Points of Interest 153

In-Depth Guide to Olympic National Park 155

  Pacific Coast 155

    Kalaloch and Ruby Beach 155
    Mora and Rialto Beach 157
    Ozette 158

  Temperate Rainforests 158

    Hoh Rainforest 159
    Quinault Rainforest 160

  Mountains and Old Growth Forests 161

    Elwha Valley 161
    Lake Crescent 162
    Sol Duc Valley 163
    Hurricane Ridge 164
    Deer Park 165
    Staircase 166

In-Depth Guide to Grand Canyon National Park 167

  South Rim 167
  Desert View 170

    Desert View Watchtower 170
    Tusayan Ruin and Museum 170

  North Rim 171
  Tuweep 172

    Toroweap Overlook 174
    Tuweep Hiking Trails 174
    Tuckup Trail 174
    Saddle Horse Loop Trail 174
    Adams Leaning Wheel Grader 175

A Final Note 176

ACKNOWLEDGEMENTS

This work would not have been possible without the support of a few very special people. I want to especially thank my dear friend Jack Tillman for all his contribution, hard work and dedication to this three book project.

I am also indebted to my brother Bobby Simms who inspired me to document my trips and start writing, who also has been supportive of my career goals and worked actively to provide me the support I needed to pursue my goals.

I am grateful to all those with whom I have had the pleasure to work with this and other related projects. Each member of my team has provided me extensive personal and professional guideline and taught me a great deal about both writing a book and publishing those works.

I would especially like to thank Denise Nicholson for her help and support in book layout, and design, without whom this monumental task would not have been done properly.

Nobody has been more important to me in the pursuit of this project than the members of my family. I would like to thank my parents, whose love and guidance are with me in whatever I pursue. They are the ultimate role models.

Most importantly, I wish to thank my loving and supportive wife Natalie, and my wonderful daughter, Liz, who always provides unending inspiration to everything I do. A special thanks to Wikipedia.org, Wikimedia.org and National Park Service for all the images and maps.

And....

To My Father, who taught me everything I know

To My Mother, without her, I won't be here

INTRODUCTION

Nothing evokes the feeling of fresh air and freedom more than visiting the great outdoors. The best way to experience the great outdoors is by traveling to one of the beautiful National Parks in the United States. Whether you are just driving through, stopping for a short day hike, or spending several days camping, there is lots to see and do in our National Parks.

Whether you enjoy the rugged outdoors or you simply want to enjoy a few scenic vistas and a museum or two, you'll find something for all fitness levels at any of these preserved natural landmarks.

Some of the parks are better known than others, but none are short on beauty and history.

In this three-volume guide, I'll take you to all the National Parks in the United States. Each guide will walk you through the basics so you can prepare for a trip to any of the locations listed with little to no trouble whatsoever. Then, I'll give you the must-see spots so you can enjoy the best of the National Parks in a single day if you don't have time to stay longer than that.

I'll also give you a few itineraries in case you have the time to take a two-week trip and want to see multiple parks along the way. I'll also go into greater detail at some of the most popular parks since you'll probably want to stay several nights and see everything the park has to offer.

So, please feel free to use this guide to plan your first or next great outdoor adventure and have fun.

PART – 1

16 NATIONAL PARKS IN THE WESTERN UNITED STATES

CHANNEL ISLANDS, CALIFORNIA

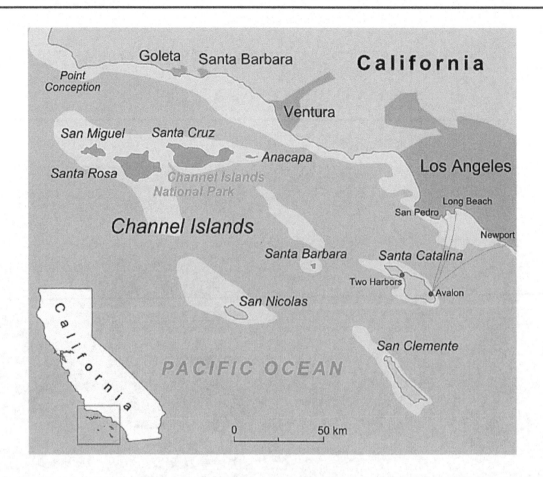

Overview

Whether your interest is in the ocean, land, or history, you'll find plenty to see and do in the vast land of the national park at the Channel Islands in California. This location is made up of five islands (San Miguel, Santa Rosa, Santa Cruz, Anacapa, and Santa Barbara) that are situated off the coast of southern California, near the bustling city of Los Angeles.

The entire national park covers 249,354 acres, out of which almost half of them are the ocean. The area was designated a US National Monument in 1938 and then became a Biosphere Reserve in 1976. It was finally established as a National Park in 1980 and today includes a marine sanctuary of six nautical miles that surround the park. Let's quickly look at the basics you need to know beforehand.

- **Visitor Centers / Hours**

    - Park is open all year, except Thanksgiving and December 25th.
    - Robert J. Lagomarsino Channel Islands National Park Visitor Center in Ventura opens at 8:30am-5: 00 pm daily.
    - Outdoors Santa Barbara Visitor Center opens at 11:00am-5:00pm daily.

- **Fees**

    - There is no cost to visit the Channel Islands, National Park.

- **Goods / Services**

    - None of the islands in the national park have goods or services available.
    - No public phone access.

- **Pets**

    - Pets are not allowed in the park in order to protect island wildlife.

- **Camping**

    - Currently, one established campground per island is available year-round:
        - Santa Barbara Island - Above the landing cove.
        - Anacapa Island - On the east islet.
        - Santa Cruz Island - At Scorpion Ranch.
        - Santa Rosa Island - At Water Canyon.
        - San Miguel Island - Above Cuyler Harbor.

- **Reservations / Permits**

- Boat and plane transportation to the island requires advanced reservations
  - For boats: Island Packers. www.islandpackers.com
  - For planes: Channel Islands Aviation. www.flycia.com
- Advanced camping reservations are required for all campgrounds.
- Reservations can be made no more than five months in advance.
- Reservations can be made through www.recreation.gov.

Wildlife

- 145 species are unique to the islands, and about 23 are terrestrial animals, including two types of island foxes specific to the islands.
- Marine life includes the endangered blue whale, the largest animal on Earth.

Weather

- Mediterranean climate year-round.
- Relatively stable temperatures with highs averaging in the mid-60s and lows in the 50s degree Fahrenheit.
- Spring features strong winds and dense fog.
- Most rain falls between December and March.

When to Visit

- Depends on what you want to see:
  - Spring is peak bloom for wildflowers and bird migration– nesting starts, the whale watching season ends, island fox pups are born, and sea lions and fur seals start to gather.
  - Summer is ideal for outdoor activities such as sailing, snorkeling, diving, kayaking, and swimming. Chicks hatch and start flying,

whale-watching begins, sea lions and fur seals start pupping. Peak visitor season is between June and August.

- ☐ Fall is when the water reaches its warmest temperature and deepest visibility. Whale watching ends, bird migration starts, elephant seals start to gather.
- ☐ Winter is when gray whale-watching starts. Elephant seals and harbor seals start pupping. Brown pelicans start nesting. Plants start blooming.

☐ **Visiting Tips**

- ☐ There are no services, so bring all the essentials.
- ☐ Enter the water at your own risk since there are no lifeguards.
- ☐ If you want to watch migrating whales, plan to visit between December and April.

DEATH VALLEY, CALIFORNIA

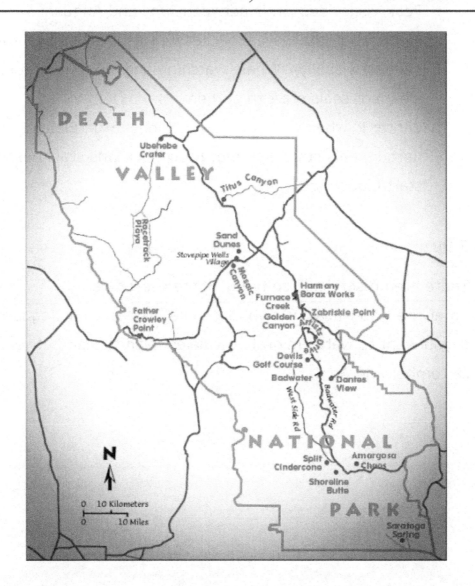

Overview

Death Valley National Park is a stark landscape to visit, especially since it is surrounded by high, snow-capped mountains. Despite the name of this national park, there are still wonderful things to enjoy.

Death Valley is the lowest point in the United States and features one of the hottest and driest landscapes. The area was first named a national monument in 1933 and was first improved by the Civilian Conservation Corps. Let's consider some of the basics you need to know before visiting this park.

- **Visitor Centers / Hours**

  - Park is open all year.
  - Furnace Creek Visitor Center and Museum open 8:00am-5:00pm daily.
  - Scotty's Castle Visitor Center was unfortunately damaged due to flooding and isn't expected to be reopened until 2020.

- **Fees**

  - Vehicle Entrance Fee of $30 for 7 days.
  - Motorcycle Entrance Fee of $25 for 7 days.
  - Individual Entrance Fee of $15 for 7 days.
  - A $55 Annual Pass may be purchased.

- **Goods / Services**

  - There are several lodging options within the park:
    - Stovepipe Wells Village - Open all year.
    - The Oasis at Death Valley: The Inn - Open all year.
    - The Oasis at Death Valley: The Ranch - Open all year.
    - Panamint Springs Resort - Open all year.
  - Most of the above lodging locations also have restaurants available.

- **Pets**

  - Pets are allowed, but with restrictions:
    - Restricted to developed areas of the park only.
    - Must be on a leash no longer than 6 feet.
    - Cannot be left unattended.
    - No more than 4 pets per campsite.
    - Pets are allowed at the Stovepipe Wells Village and Panamint Springs Resort for an extra fee.

- **Camping**

    - Backcountry camping is permitted throughout the parks wilderness areas.
    - In developed campgrounds, there is a limit of 15 people and 6 vehicles.

        - Furnace Creek - Open All Year - $18
        - Sunset - Open October to April - $12
        - Texas Spring - Open October to April - $14
        - Stovepipe Wells - Open October to April - $12
        - Mesquite Spring - Open All Year - $12
        - Emigrant - Tent Only - Open All Year - Free
        - Wildrose - Open All Year - Free
        - Thorndike - Open March to November - Free
        - Mahogany Flat - Open March to November – Free

- **Reservations / Permits**

    - Reservations can be made through www.recreation.gov.

- **Wildlife**

    - Wildlife ranges from bighorn sheep to mountain lions.
    - There is an abundance of butterfly species.

- **Weather**

    - One of the hottest and driest areas in the United States.
    - Summer temperatures can often reach 120 degrees Fahrenheit in the shade with overnight lows in the 90s.
    - The average rainfall is less than 2 inches, and late summer thunderstorms can cause flash flooding.

☐ Winter and spring can be pleasant with mild temperatures. However, sudden dust storms can occur in spring.

☐ **When to Visit**

  ☐ The park can be visited year-round, but winter months tend to be the best time to visit.

☐ **Visiting Tips**

  ☐ No matter what time of the year you visit, be sure to bring lots of water and drink at least a gallon or more a day depending on your activity level. Also, make it a point to consume salty foods as to retain more water.

  ☐ Watch where you step and reach to avoid rattlesnakes, scorpions, and black widow spiders.

  ☐ Avoid canyons in rainstorms due to potential flash flooding.

  ☐ Avoid mine shafts and tunnels for safety.

JOSHUA TREE, CALIFORNIA

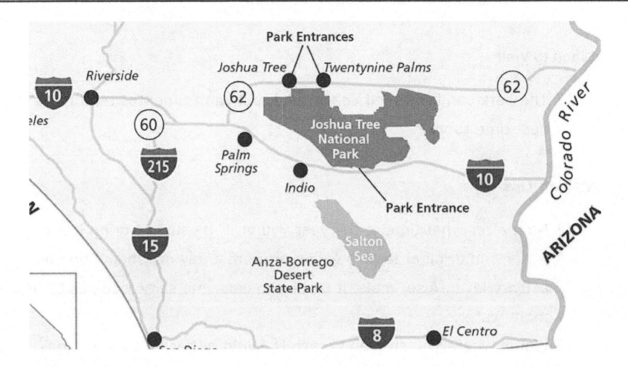

Overview

The Joshua Tree is a distinct and unique plant, and you can find them in abundance at the Joshua Tree National Park. This national park is over 800,000 acres of beautiful landscape that was created by a combination of torrential rain, wind, and extreme temperatures. There are several ecosystems that thrive in this area and can be enjoyed by visitors of all ages.

☐ **Visitor Centers / Hours**

- ☐ Park is open all year.
- ☐ Joshua Tree Visitor Center at the West Entrance opens at 8:00am-5:00pm daily.
- ☐ Oasis Visitor Center in Twentynine Palms opens at 8:30am-5:00pm daily.
- ☐ Cottonwood Visitor Center at the South Entrance opens at 8:30am-4:00pm daily.

☐ Black Rock Nature Center in the Black Rock Campground opens October to May 8:00am-4:00pm.

☐ **Fees**

    ☐ Vehicle Entrance Fee of $30 for 7 days.

    ☐ Motorcycle Entrance Fee of $25 for 7 days.

    ☐ Individual Entrance Fee of $15 for 7 days.

    ☐ A $55 Annual Pass may be purchased.

☐ **Goods / Services**

    ☐ Water is only available at a few locations within the park:

        ☐ Oasis Visitor Center in Twentynine Palms.

        ☐ West Entrance Station

        ☐ Black Rock Campground

        ☐ Cottonwood Campground

        ☐ Indian Cove Ranger Station

    ☐ There is no other place to get food, gas, water, lodging, or other services in the park.

    ☐ Very few areas of the park have cell phone coverage.

☐ **Pets**

    ☐ Pets are allowed, but with restrictions:

        ☐ Pets must be within 100 feet of roads, picnic areas, and campgrounds.

        ☐ Pets must be on a leash no longer than 6 feet at all times.

    ✱ Not allowed on any trails

- **Camping**

  - In summer months; campgrounds are on a first come, first served basis:

    - Belle - $15
    - Black Rock - $20
    - Cottonwood - $20
    - Hidden Valley - $15
    - Indian Cove - $20
    - Jumbo Rocks - $15
    - Ryan - $15
    - White Tank - $15

- **Reservations / Permits**

  - No reservations are required for Joshua Tree National Park.

- **Wildlife**

  - You'll find large herds of bighorn sheep, black-tailed jackrabbits, coyotes, and kangaroo rats.
  - During the winter months, you'll find a wind range of migratory birds.

- **Weather**

  - Weather is best in spring and fall; during these seasons, daytime temperatures are in the mid-80s and drop to the low 50s at night.
  - Summer temperatures can rise to the 100s in the daytime and mid-70s at night.

☐ **When to Visit**

   ☐ The park can be visited year-round, but spring and fall are when visitors reach their peak.

☐ **Visiting Tips**

   ☐ If you travel in the summer, make sure you hike early in the day as to avoid most of the harsh sunshine.

   ☐ Travel in the spring if you want to see wildflowers in bloom and discover how colorful the desert really is.

   ☐ Twilight is the best time for photos.

   ☐ Early morning is when you are most likely to spot coyotes.

   ☐ Make sure you pack the essentials since there are limited services in the park.

   ☐ Enjoy a great meal at the Crossroad Cafe in Joshua Tree or the Joshua Tree Saloon.

SEQUOIA & KINGS, CALIFORNIA

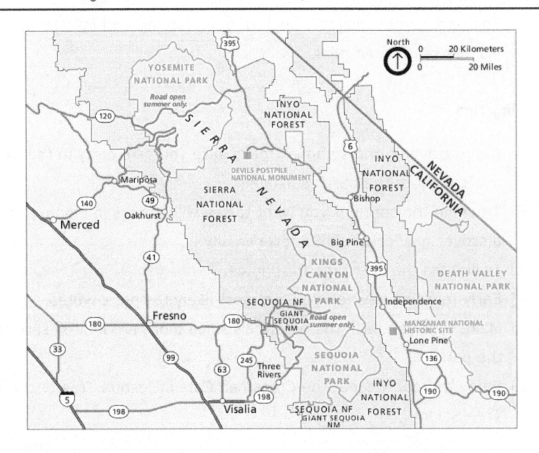

Overview

Sequoia and Kings National Parks are two adjoining parks that feature the colossal redwood trees. Sequoia National Park also allows a glimpse into history since it was the second national park in the United States. Both parks feature a variation in landscapes that provide a rich variety of habitats to explore. Sequoia was established as a National Park in 1890, and Kings was established in 1940.

- **Visitor Centers / Hours**

    - Park is open all year.
    - Foothills Visitor Center north of the Ash Mountain Entrance opens at 8:00am-4:30pm daily.
    - Kings Canyon Visitor Center opens at 9:00am-4:00pm daily.
    - Lodgepole Visitor Center opens at 7:00am-5:00pm daily.

☐ Cedar Grove Visitor Center opens at 9:00am-5:00pm daily.

☐ **Fees**

    ☐ Vehicle Entrance Fee of $35 for 1-7 days.

    ☐ Motorcycle Entrance Fee of $30 for 1-7 days.

    ☐ Individual Entrance Fee of $20 for 1-7 days.

    ☐ A $60 Annual Pass may be purchased.

☐ **Goods / Services**

    ☐ Commercial services within the park include restaurants, snack bars, markets, gift shops, and lodging. Some of these locations provide Wi-Fi.

    ☐ Very few areas of the park have cell phone coverage.

☐ **Pets**

    ☐ Pets aren't allowed on the trails.

    ☐ Pets in campgrounds and picnic areas need to be on a leash at all times.

☐ **Camping**

    ☐ Together there are 14 campgrounds in these two parks; three are open year-round.

    ☐ Most campsites are first come, first served.

    ☐ Standard campsites allow up to 6 people.

☐ **Reservations / Permits**

    ☐ No reservations are required for both parks.

- **Wildlife**

  - Year-round and seasonal animals are seen in both parks. This goes from gray fox and bobcats to marmots and pikas.

- **Weather**

  - Summers tend to be hot and dry, while winters are cold and snowy at higher elevations.

- **When to Visit**

  - The park can be visited year-round, but certain roads can be closed due to snow and rain.

- **Visiting Tips**

  - For overnight backpacking, you will need a wilderness permit. During the busy season, these are limited, but there is no limit from October to late May.
  - Always take precautions for bears, even if you are just there for a day picnic. Pro-tip: bears dislike loud noises, and as long as one throws their food away properly and stays away from the bear territory, there ought to be no unpleasant encounters with these large, furry mammals.

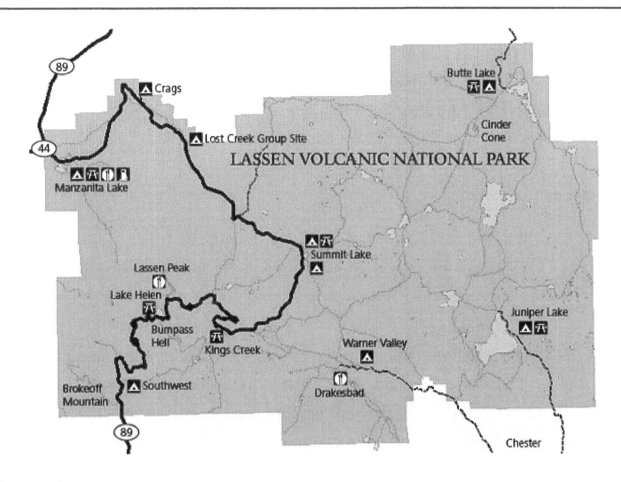

Overview

This park was established in 1916 in Northern California and is a peaceful forest and wilderness adventure full of hissing fumaroles and mud pots. It is also a wonderful place to visit for those who want to view untouched wilderness that is still changing the landscape today.

☐ **Visitor Centers / Hours**

    ☐ Park is open all year.

    ☐ Kohm Yah-mah-nee Visitor Center is open seasonally 9:00am-5:00pm.

- **Fees**

  - Vehicle Entrance Fee of $25 for 1-7 days.
  - Winter Pass $10 for 1-7 days.
  - Motorcycle Entrance Fee of $20 for 1-7 days.
  - Individual Entrance Fee of $12 for 1-7 days.
  - A $50 Annual Pass may be purchased.

- **Goods / Services**

  - Within the park, there are two lodging options:
    - Drakesbad Guest Ranch - open early June through October
    - Manzanita Lake Camping Cabins - open mid-May through October
  - There are three options within the park for stores, food, and gasoline:
    - Lassen Cafe and Gift is located in the Kohm Yah-mah-nee Visitor Center and is open in the summer months
    - The Manzanita Lake Camper Store is open mid-May through mid-October and also offers gasoline
  - Coin-operated showers are available at the Manzanita Lake Camper Store.
  - Cell phone coverage is spotty within the park.

- **Pets**

  - Pets aren't allowed on the trails.
  - Pets in campgrounds and picnic areas need to be on a leash at all times.

- **Camping**

  - There are eight campgrounds at Lassen Volcanic, and they range from developed to primitive.

☐ Half of the campsites require reservations and the other half are first come, first served.

☐ Reservations / Permits

☐ Certain campgrounds can be reserved through www.reservation.org

☐ A wilderness camping permit is required for backcountry camping.

☐ A stock day use permit is required if bringing in a horse or any other pack animals.

☐ Wildlife

☐ Year-round and seasonal animals are seen in both parks.

☐ Weather

☐ Weather tends to fall into one of two categories: winter and summer.

☐ Winter weather conditions occur between November to May.

☐ Summer weather conditions occur between June to October.

☐ Snowstorms have been known to happen as late as June.

☐ When to Visit

☐ The park can be visited year-round, but certain roads can be closed due to snow and rain.

☐ Visiting Tips

☐ The park has five separate entrances and only one main road that runs north-south through the park.

☐ It is recommended you don't use GPS units for directions in the park since they are often incorrect; instead, you should rely on maps and road signs.

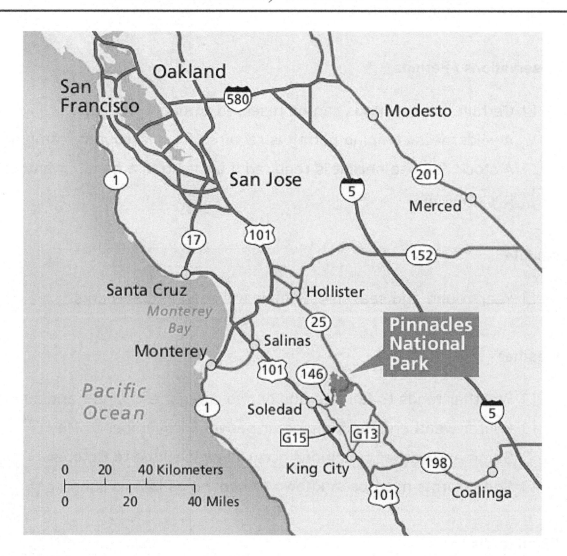

Overview

This national park was created as a result of an ancient volcanic eruption, and you can explore 26,000 acres of wildlands rich in diverse wildlife and spring wildflowers as a result. The park was given full national park status in 2013.

- **Visitor Centers / Hours**

  - Park is open all year.
  - Pinnacles Visitor Center is open daily from 9:30am-5:00pm.

☐ West Pinnacles Visitor Contact Station is open daily from 9:00am-4:30pm.

☐ **Fees**

☐ Vehicle Entrance Fee of $25.

☐ Motorcycle Entrance Fee of $20.

☐ Individual Entrance Fee of $12.

☐ A $50 Annual Pass may be purchased.

☐ **Goods / Services**

☐ There are no services available in the park.

☐ **Pets**

☐ Pets aren't allowed on the trails.

☐ Pets in campgrounds and picnic areas need to be on a leash at all times.

☐ **Camping**

☐ There is one campground: Pinnacles Campground.

☐ **Reservations / Permits**

☐ Campsites can be reserved through www.reservation.org

☐ **Wildlife**

☐ Year-round and seasonal animals are seen in the park.

☐ **Weather**

    ☐ The park has a Mediterranean climate with hot and dry summers and mild winters with moderate precipitation.

☐ **When to Visit**

    ☐ The park can be visited year-round, but spring and fall provide the best times to visit and hike the park.

☐ **Visiting Tips**

    ☐ Be sure to bring a headlamp or flashlight with you to explore caves.

    ☐ Consider visiting the park at night for clear stargazing and a better chance at spotting wildlife.

    ☐ Hike to the High Peaks in early morning or evening for your best chance to see the California condors.

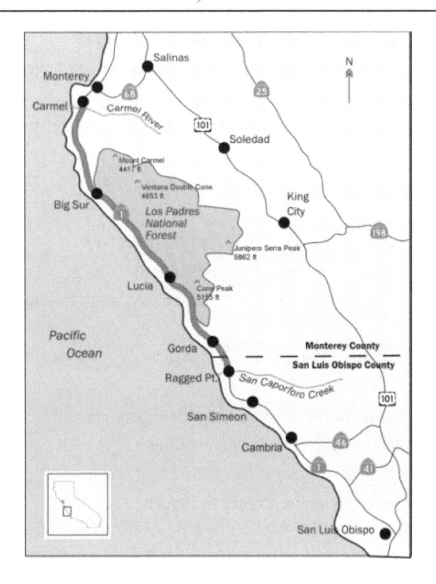

REDWOOD, CALIFORNIA

Overview

The Redwood tree is a beautiful creation of nature, dating back to the times of the Roman Empire. You'll see some of the oldest and tallest redwood trees at the Redwood National Park in California, established in 1968. This park features prairie, woodland, river, and coastline habitats.

- **Visitor Centers / Hours**

    - Park is open all year.

☐ Crescent City Visitor Center in Crescent City, CA

   ☐ Spring to Fall open daily 9:00am-5:00pm
   ☐ Winter open 9:00am-4:00pm and is closed Tuesday and Wednesday
   ☐ Closed on New Year's, Thanksgiving, and Christmas Day

☐ Thomas H. Kuchel Visitor Center in Orick, CA

   ☐ Spring to Fall open daily 9:00am-5:00pm
   ☐ Winter open daily 9:00am-4:00pm
   ☐ Closed on New Year's, Thanksgiving and Christmas Day

☐ Hiouchi Visitor Center in Hiouchi, CA

   ☐ Spring to fall open daily 9:00am-5:00pm
   ☐ Winter open daily 9:00am-4:00pm

☐ Jedediah Smith Visitor Center in Hiouchi, CA

   ☐ Open May 31 through September 30 daily at 9:00am-5:00pm

☐ Prairie Creek Visitor Center

   ☐ Summer open daily 9:00am-5:00pm
   ☐ Off-Season and Winter open daily 9:00am-4:00pm
   ☐ Closed on New Year's, Thanksgiving, and Christmas Day.

☐ **Fees**

☐ The National Park is free to enter.

- Jedediah Smith, Del Norte Coast, and Prairie Creek Redwoods State Parks collect day use fees at the campground entrances.
- Gold Bluffs Beach and Fern Canyon require a day use fee.

Goods / Services

- There are no services available in the park.

Pets

- Pets aren't allowed on the trails.
- Pets in campgrounds, beaches, and gravel roads need to be on a leash at all times.

Camping

- There are 4 developed campgrounds in the park and all cost $35:
  - Jedediah Smith, Mill Creek, Elk Prairie, and Gold Bluffs Beach.

Reservations / Permits

- Campsites can be reserved through www.reservecalifornia.com

Wildlife

- Year-round and seasonal animals are seen in the park. The most visible are sea lions and gray whales. When traveling in the prairies, you may be likely to see Roosevelt elk. Commonly seen birds are pelicans, ospreys, and gulls.

Weather

- The winter months from October to April come with a lot of precipitation.

- ☐ The location near the California coast keeps the temperature between 40 and 60 degrees Fahrenheit year-round.
- ☐ The further inland you go, the warmer and drier the weather becomes.

☐ When to Visit

- ☐ The park can be visited year-round.

☐ Visiting Tips

- ☐ Mid-May to early June is the ideal time to view the native Rhododendron flowers.
- ☐ There are three private attractions in the area that allow you to drive through a redwood tree.
- ☐ When planning a trip to the area or camping, be sure to be prepared for black bears, mountain lions, ticks, and poison oak. While the Roosevelt Elk is used to humans, they can be dangerous during the rut and calving seasons.

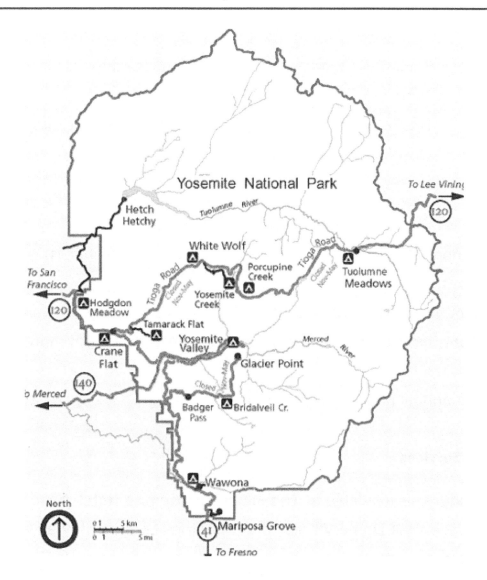

Overview

Yosemite National Park, established in 1890, is one of the most popular national parks in the United States– it is visited by nearly four million people every year, so they would probably agree. Here you will find breathtaking vistas, beautiful hiking trails, and plenty of vacation opportunities to keep you busy for days. Yosemite is also a land of history since it was the first national land dedicated to recreation.

☐ **Visitor Centers / Hours**

- Park is open all year.
- There are two main entrances to the park:

  - Tioga Pass Entrance is closed from November until late May or June.
  - Hetch Hetchy Entrance is open year-round but may occasionally close due to snow.

- **Fees**

  - A non-commercial vehicle with 15 or fewer passengers: $35 for 7 days.
  - Motorcycle: $30 for 7 days.
  - Foot, bicycle, horse, or non-commercial vehicle with more than 15 passengers: $20 for 7 days.
  - An annual pass is available for $70.

- **Goods / Services**

  - Lodging is available at The Majestic Yosemite Hotel, Yosemite Valley Lodge, Half Dome Village, and Big Trees Lodge– they all have internet access.
  - Many locations and villages in the park offer full services including gas, groceries, and other needed services for travelers.

- **Pets**

  - Pets are allowed in developed areas, on fully-paved roads, sidewalks, bicycle paths, and in all campsites except walk-in campsites and group campsites.
  - Pet must be on a leash not over six feet or physically restrained in some way.

- **Camping**

  - Yosemite is divided into three areas with several campsites each. Fees and operating hours vary:

    - Yosemite Valley

      - Upper Pines - Open all year - $26
      - Lower Pines - Open March 30 to October 26 - $26
      - North Pines - Open March 26 to November 12 - $26
      - Camp 4 - Open all year - $6/person - first come, first served

    - South of Yosemite Valley

      - Wawona - Open all year - $26
      - Bridalveil Creek - Open July 1 to July 19 - $18 - first come, first served

    - North of Yosemite Valley

      - Hodgdon Meadow - Open all year - $26
      - Crane Flat - Open May 25 to October 15 - $26
      - Tamarack Flat - Open June 2 to October 15 - $12 - first come, first served.
      - White Wolf - Open July 13 to October 1 - $18 - first come, first served.
      - Yosemite Creek - Open June 28 to September 4 - $12 - first come, first served.
      - Porcupine Flat - Open July 6 to October 15 - $12 - first come, first served.

- Tuolumne Meadows - Open June 14 to September 24 - $26

☐ **Reservations / Permits**

    ☐ You can make reservations through www.recreation.gov

☐ **Wildlife**

    ☐ Nearly 400 animal species call Yosemite their home. Common mammals seen in the park include black bears, mule deer, and foxes. At the northeastern part of the park, you'll sometimes see the endangered Sierra Nevada bighorn sheep. The park also hosts large seasonal populations of birds including spotted owls or great gray owls.

☐ **Weather**

    ☐ The weather in Yosemite varies throughout the year. May to September are summer months with minimal rainfall; high temperatures are in the upper 70s to low 90 degrees Fahrenheit. In the summer months, low temperatures can drop into the 40s category. Spring is the rainy season at the park, and temperatures often range from the low 30s to the upper 60s. Winter typically features rapid snowstorms that last for days and coat the park with a heavy layer of snow.

☐ **When to Visit**

    ☐ The park can be visited year-round.

☐ **Visiting Tips**

☐ Yosemite is a very popular park, and you should ensure you make reservations months in advance. Visit in the late fall or winter if you want fewer crowds and easier reservations.

☐ While there are lots of modern amenities at the park, cell phone service is still spotty at best, so always carry a paper map with you.

☐ Consider taking one of the free shuttles that operate year-round to avoid the hassle of finding parking.

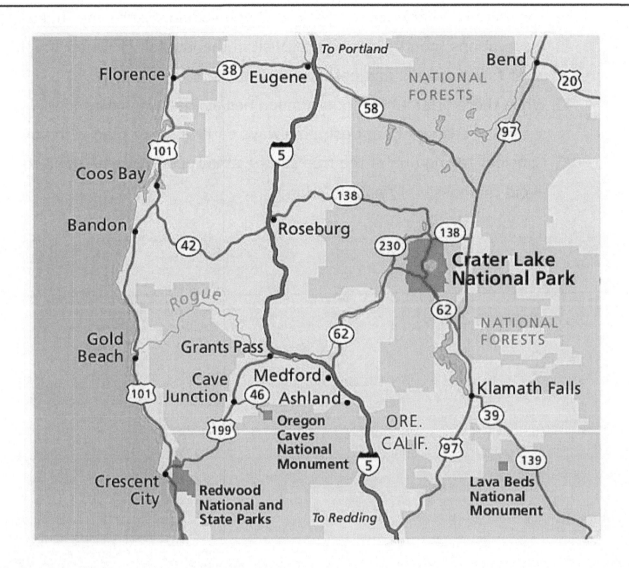

Overview

At Crater Lake National Park you get to view a dormant volcano with a beautiful blue lake, which is the deepest one in the United States standing at 1,943 feet. Around the lake are 183,224 acres of stunning evergreen forests.

- **Visitor Centers / Hours**

  - Park is open all year, but some roads, trails, and facilities are open seasonally due to snow.
  - Steel Visitor Center at Park Headquarters - Open Year-Round.

☐ Rim Visitor Center - Opens May 25

☐ **Fees**

    ☐ Cars: $25 in summer (May 13 to October 31) $10 in winter (November 1 to May 12)

    ☐ Motorcycles: $20 in summer (May 13 to October 31) $10 in winter (November 1 to May 12)

    ☐ Bicycles and Pedestrians: $12 per individual

☐ **Goods / Services**

    ☐ Lodging is available at two locations:

        ☐ Crater Lake Lodge - Opens May 18

        ☐ The Cabins at Mazama Village - Opens May 25

    ☐ Food:

        ☐ Rim Village Cafe - Open Year-Round

        ☐ Crater Lake Lodge Dining Room - Open May 18

        ☐ Annie Creek Restaurant - Open May 25

☐ **Pets**

    ☐ Pets are only allowed on paved roads, parking lots, and within 50 feet of these areas.

    ☐ Leashes can only be six feet long at maximum.

    ☐ Only one pet per hiker is allowed.

    ☐ Pets are only allowed on the following trails:

        ☐ The Godfrey Glen Trail

        ☐ The Lady of the Woods Trail

        ☐ The Grayback Drive

☐ The Pacific Crest Trail

☐ Pets aren't allowed in park buildings.

☐ **Camping**

☐ Crater Lake National Park has two developed campgrounds that are only open in summer:

☐ Mazama Campground takes reservations except in June. Costs $22 to $31.

☐ Lost Creek Campground is a first come, first served campground only. Cost $10.

☐ Backcountry camping is allowed year-round, but heavy snowfall can happen in winter months.

☐ **Reservations / Permits**

☐ You can make reservations through www.recreation.gov

☐ **Wildlife**

☐ Due to its water sources, Crater Lake National Park is home to multiple species ranging from black bears and coyotes to hummingbirds and chipmunks.

☐ **Weather**

☐ Winters are long and snowy with an average snowfall of 43 feet per year.

☐ Summers are short but often sunny and warm.

☐ May, June, and October feature sunny days with intermittent periods of rain and snow.

☐ **When to Visit**

☐ The park can be visited year-round. For dry, warm weather your best times to visit are July, August, and September.

☐ **Visiting Tips**

☐ Since campgrounds are limited, be sure to book early if you want to visit in the peak summer season. For a cheaper camping option or as a backup, consider the nearby Rogue River National Forest.

☐ No matter what time of the year you travel in, you'll need warm gear since the caldera is foggy all the time and weather can be unpredictable.

Overview

Mount Rainier is one of the most visited national parks in the United States, as well as the most prominent peak of the Cascade Range. Established in 1899, it is also one of the oldest national parks in the United States. The mountain is still an active volcano but hasn't erupted in over 150 years.

☐ **Visitor Centers / Hours**

☐ The park is open year-round.

☐ Henry M. Jackson Memorial Visitor Center at Paradise, Washington is open year-round, but only on weekends in winter. It is open at the following times:

  ☐ June 16 - September 23, 10:00am-7:00pm daily.
  ☐ September 24 - October 8, 10:00am-5:00pm daily.
  ☐ October 13 - 28, 10:00am-5:00pm weekends only.
  ☐ November 3 - December 31, 10:00am-4:15pm weekends and holidays only.

☐ Ohanapecosh Visitor Center. Open late June through September:

  ☐ May 25 - September 16, 9:00am-5:00pm daily.
  ☐ September 21 - October 7, 9:00am-5:00pm Friday to Sunday.

☐ Sunrise Visitor Center. Open July through mid-September:

  ☐ 10:00am-6:00pm daily.

☐ **Fees**

  ☐ Single Vehicle Fee: $30
  ☐ Per person fee for walk-ups and bicycles: $15
  ☐ Motorcycle Fee: $25
  ☐ Annual Pass: $55

☐ **Goods / Services**

  ☐ There are three options for lodging in the park:

    ☐ Paradise Inn
    ☐ National Park Inn

- Sunrise Day Lodge

- Food is available at these locations.
- There is no gas or other services located within the park.

Pets

- Pets are allowed in the park, but not in the following areas:

  - Trails, with the exception of the Pacific Crest Trail
  - Wilderness and/or off-trail areas
  - In park buildings
  - On snow-covered roads closed for winter

- Pets must always be on a leash no longer than six feet.
- Pets must always be under the control of their owner.
- Owners must clean up after their pets.

Camping

- Campground fees are $20 per night.
- There are four campgrounds in the park:

  - Cougar Rock open late May to September
  - Ohanapecosh open late May to September
  - White River open late June to September
  - Mowich Lake open early July to October

Reservations / Permits

- You can make reservations through www.recreation.gov for Cougar Rock and Ohanapecosh campsites. All others are first come, first served.

- **Wildlife**

  - The size of the park means a great diversity of wildlife can be observed. The elevation you are at will determine the specific animals you see. At the foothills, for example, you are most likely to see deer, squirrels, and jays.

- **Weather**

  - The general weather in the park is rainy and cool, even into July and August.
  - You should bring rain gear year-round.
  - The weather on the mountain near the peak is ever-changing and unpredictable, so make sure to be prepared by equipping yourself with all types of weather possibilities.

- **When to Visit**

  - The park can be visited year-round.

- **Visiting Tips**

  - If you want to backpack in the park, you'll need a wilderness permit, and if you want to climb above 10,000 feet, you'll need a climbing pass.
  - Be aware of the avalanche risk and head uphill if you hear a sound like an oncoming train.

NORTH CASCADES, WASHINGTON

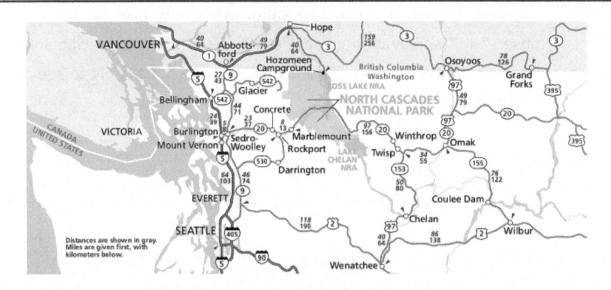

Overview

At the North Cascades National Park, you can view everything from jagged peaks to forested valleys and glaciers, to waterways. The North Cascades mountain range was established as a national park in 1968 and is often referred to as the North American Alps.

- **Visitor Centers / Hours**

    - The park is open year-round, but the weather will dictate when specific facilities and roads are open.
    - North Cascades Visitor Center is open May 18 to September 30, 9:00am-5:00pm daily.
    - Golden West Visitor Center is open May 25 to October 13, 8:30am-5:00pm daily.

- **Fees**

    - There is no cost to visit North Cascades National Park.

- **Goods / Services**

  - There are a lot of options for accommodations and food services within the National Park area.

- **Pets**

  - Pets are not allowed in the national park with the exception of the Pacific Crest Trail and within 50 feet of roads.
  - Pets on a leash are allowed within Ross Lake and Lake Chelan National Recreation Areas.

- **Camping**

  - Campground fees are $16 per night. Except for Gorge Lake and Hozomeen Campgrounds, which are free.
  - There are a number of campgrounds and car campground options at North Cascades National Park, and their availability is based on the weather– so you should contact the park to find out availability before planning a trip.

- **Reservations / Permits**

  - You can make reservations through www.recreation.gov, and other campgrounds are first come, first served.

- **Wildlife**

  - The park is home to many larger species such as bears, wolves, elk, mountain goats, moose, deer, and coyotes. Because of the risk involved in approaching these creatures, it is extremely important to remember proper cautionary techniques.

☐ **Weather**

    ☐ Storms are common in the area, so always come prepared for wind and rain.

    ☐ Heavy snow and rain are common at higher elevations in the winter.

    ☐ Avalanches can occur in winter and spring, so use caution around steep mountain slopes.

    ☐ The east side of the mountains is warmer and drier in the summer than the west side.

☐ **When to Visit**

    ☐ The park can be visited year-round.

    ☐ The best time to visit is mid-June to late September.

    ☐ Autumn and spring are the best times for car tours.

☐ **Visiting Tips**

    ☐ Be prepared at all times– even summer can have unexpected storms.

    ☐ All overnight stays will require a backcountry camping permit.

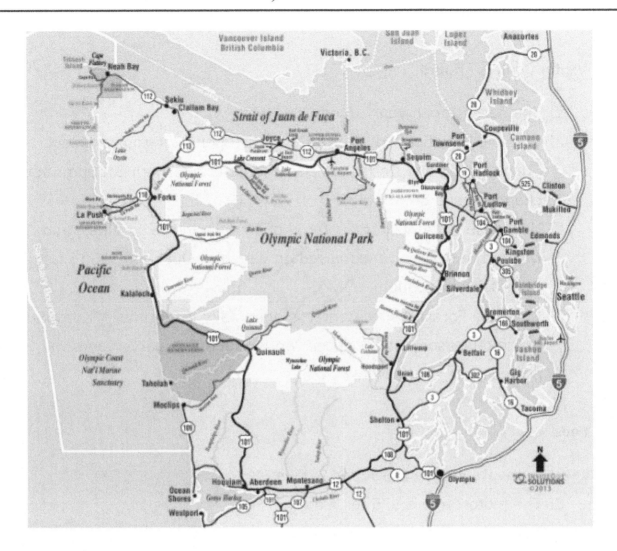

Overview

At Olympic National Park you are able to experience all aspects of the Pacific Northwest, from the breathtaking coastal views to the crisp mountain air, and even a tropical rainforest. Established as a National Park in 1909, it was officially renamed the Olympic National Park by President Franklin Roosevelt in 1938. It was then named an International Biosphere Reserve in 1976 and a World Heritage Site in 1981.

Within the almost one million acres of the park, there are three distinct ecosystems including glacier mountains, a rugged coastline, and temperate forests. It is one of the largest wilderness areas in the lower 48 states. As you can imagine, this park is ideal for the adventurer type of hiker.

- **Visitor Centers / Hours**

  - The park is open year-round.
  - Olympic National Park Visitor Center is open year-round except Thanksgiving and Christmas Day. Hours are 8:30am-5:00pm, but may change based on weather.
  - Hurricane Ridge Visitor Center is open daily in the summer, and the rest of the season varies based on weather. Open May 25 to October 14, 10:00am-5:30pm.
  - Hoh Rain Forest Visitor Center is open daily in summer, Friday-Sunday in the offseason, and is closed January and February. Hours will vary according to the season.

- **Fees**

  - A private vehicle is $30 for 7 days.
  - The motorcycle is $25 for 7 days.
  - Per person is $15 for 7 days.

- **Goods / Services**

  - There are limited services at some of the visitor's centers.

- **Pets**

  - Pets are allowed on the following trails:

    - Peabody Creek Trail
    - Rialto Beach parking lot to Ellen Creek
    - The beaches between the Hoh and Quinault Reservations

☐ Madison Falls Trail

☐ Spruce Railroad Trail

☐ July Creek Loop Trail

☐ Pets are also allowed in campgrounds, picnic areas, and paved or dirt roads as long as they don't roll or dig in plants.

☐ **Camping**

☐ Campground fees are $8 per person per night for wilderness camping, and campgrounds range from $15-$22.

☐ Kalaloch and Sol Duc are the only campgrounds accepting reservations in summer. All other campgrounds are first come, first served.

☐ Deer Park Campground open June to mid-October for a $15 fee.

☐ Dosewallips Campground opens all year– no fee.

☐ Fairholme Campground opens April 27 to October 1 at a fee of $20, along with an added $10 to use the dump station

☐ Graves Creek Campground open year-round at $20.

☐ Heart O' the Hills Campground open year-round at $20.

☐ Hoh Campground open year-round for $20.

☐ Kalaloch Campground open year-round and requires a $22 fee, including an extra $10 to use the dump station

☐ Mora Campground open year-round for $20, and $10 more to use the dump station.

☐ North Fork Campground open year-round, $15.

☐ Ozette Campground open year-round, $20.

☐ Queets Campground open year-round, $15.

☐ Sol Duc Campground open March 23 to October 29, $21 plus tax if walk-in, $24 plus tax if reserved, $10 per use of dump station.

☐ South Beach Campground open May 18 to September 24, $15.

☐ Staircase Campground open year-round, but primitive in winter $20.

- **Reservations / Permits**

  - Wilderness camping permits are required for all overnight stays in the park.
  - Reservations are needed for all backcountry/wilderness areas.
  - Contact the park for your permits and reservations.

- **Wildlife**

  - The three ecosystems in Olympic National Park means it has a diversity of wildlife. You'll have the opportunity to view sea otters, whales, beavers, bears, rhinoceros auklets, golden eagles, deer, and moose. The park is also home to a species of marmot and salamander that can't be found anywhere else.

- **Weather**

  - Due to its size, you are likely to experience two different climates at the same time while visiting the park.
  - In the mountains, the weather is often unpredictable and constantly changing.
  - Weather can range from extreme cold to bright hot sun, so you should come prepared for both.

- **When to Visit**

  - The park can be visited year-round.

- **Visiting Tips**

  - Several roads are prone to washouts and access can be limited to some areas at times. Check with the park for current road updates.
  - The best sunsets are viewed from Ruby Beach, and the Shi Shi Beach, which is considerably more difficult to get to.

- It is best to take 3 to 5 days to view everything the park has to offer.
- No roads cross this location– Highway 101 circles the park, which takes you a half a day to cover by car.

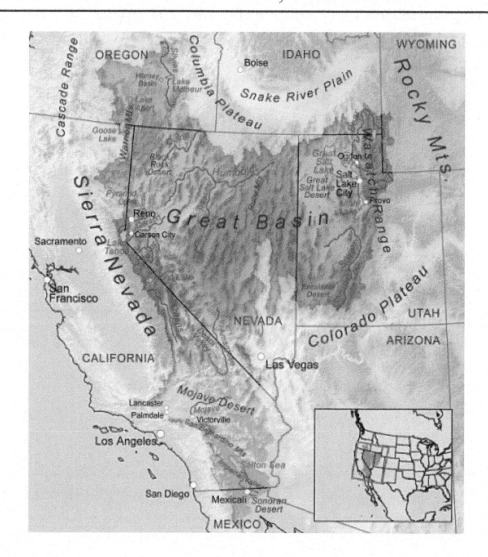

Overview

This is the only National Park in the state of Nevada. It features bristlecone pine trees, a diverse and rich wildlife, and a range of caverns and caves. The park is located between the Sierra Nevada and the Wasatch Mountains in an area known as the Great Basin. It is so remote that it is one of the darkest places in the United States, making it well-known for its astronomy programs.

☐ **Visitor Centers / Hours**

☐ The park is open year-round.

- Lehman Caves Visitor Center open daily 8:00am-5:00pm in the summer and 8:00am-4:30pm in the fall and spring; closed New Years Day, Thanksgiving Day, and Christmas Day.
- Great Basin Visitor Center open daily 8:00am-5:30pm in the summer and closed in the fall to spring.

Fees

- There is no fee to enter the park.

Goods / Services

- There are no goods or services available in the park.

Pets

- Pets are not allowed in backcountry areas of the park or on trails, with the exception of the Lexington Arch Trail and the trail between Baker and the Great Basin Visitors Center.
- Leashed pets are only allowed in campgrounds, in front of visitor centers, and on paved roads.
- Leashes cannot be any longer than six feet.
- Pets must be cleaned up after.

Camping

- Campground fees are $15 per night.
- There are several primitive campgrounds that are free, but it is recommended that you register beforehand so they can track visitors.
- There are five developed campgrounds:

    - Upper Lehman Creek
    - Lower Lehman Creek

☐ Baker Creek

☐ Grey Cliffs

☐ Wheeler Park

☐ Lower Lehman Creek is the only campground open year-round. All other campgrounds are generally open May through October.

☐ **Reservations / Permits**

☐ Permits aren't necessary for background camping, but it is recommended that you register.

☐ All campsites are first come, first served, except for Grey Cliffs Campground, which is open from May to the end of September. Reservations can be made at www.recreation.gov

☐ **Wildlife**

☐ There is a great variety of wildlife to view while visiting the park.

☐ **Weather**

☐ Weather in the park varies based on elevation.

☐ In late spring and early summer, the valley days are hot, and the snowpack may not have melted at higher elevations.

☐ Strong afternoon thunderstorms are common in the summer.

☐ At higher elevations, snow storms can occur at any time throughout the year.

☐ **When to Visit**

☐ The park can be visited year-round.

☐ **Visiting Tips**

☐ There is an additional fee to visit Lehman Caves; it is recommended to call ahead for reservations.

☐ Visit the Magic Grove for the largest grouping of the bristlecone pine.

☐ Dress in layers and pack for different climates.

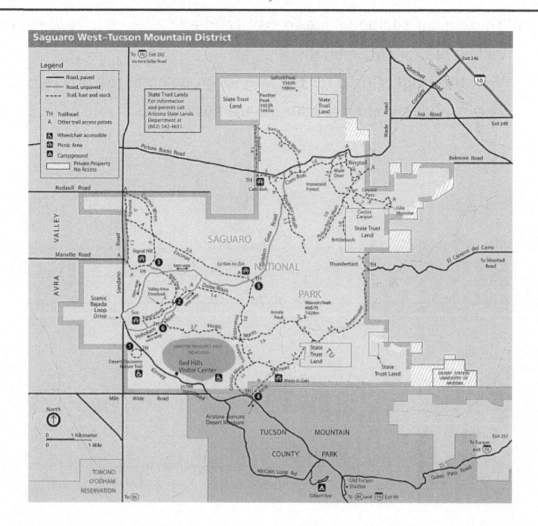

Overview

This national park protects the largest cacti species, the saguaro. Here you'll find plenty of outdoor activities for any experience level. The park is located just outside the city of Tucson in Arizona and is a wonderful place to visit in order to experience the heat of the desert and the magnificent, subtropical giant cacti.

- ☐ **Visitor Centers / Hours**

  - ☐ You can walk or bike into the park at any time.
  - ☐ The West District of the park is open to vehicles from sunrise to sunset.

- ☐ The East District of the park is open to vehicles from 7:00am to sunset.
- ☐ Both districts have a visitor center that is open every day except Christmas Day and is open 9:00am-5:00pm daily.

☐ **Fees**

- ☐ Passes are good for 7 days and are valid for both park districts.
  - ☐ $15 per vehicle
  - ☐ $10 per motorcycle
  - ☐ $5 per person
- ☐ An annual pass is available for $35

☐ **Goods / Services**

- ☐ There are no services available in either district, and there are no drive-in campgrounds.

☐ **Pets**

- ☐ Pets are only allowed on roadways, picnic areas (with the exception of Mam-A-Gah picnic area in the Western District), and paved roads.
- ☐ Pets must be on a leash no longer than six feet.

☐ **Camping**

- ☐ There are six designated campgrounds none accommodate vehicles and must be hiked to.

  - ☐ Manning Camp
  - ☐ Spud Rock Spring
  - ☐ Happy Valley Saddle
  - ☐ Juniper Basin

☐ Douglas Spring

☐ **Reservations / Permits**

　☐ Backcountry camping is available by permit. Permits can be obtained two months in advance and no later than noon on the day of your trip.

　☐ A permit is required for all overnight stays at designated campgrounds. The cost is $8 per night, per campsite.

☐ **Wildlife**

　☐ There are hundreds of different creatures to view while visiting the park. You can count on approximately 70 mammal species, 50 reptile species, and 200 bird species. Gila monsters, kangaroo rats, roadrunners, horned lizards, and rattlesnakes are only a few examples.

☐ **Weather**

　☐ Summers can be very hot with temperatures as high as 105 degrees Fahrenheit in the shade; nights only go as low as 72 degrees.

　☐ Winters offer mild warm days of about 65 degrees and cooler nights of about 40 degrees.

☐ **When to Visit**

　☐ The park can be visited year-round, but come prepared with lots of water and electrolytes if you are going to visit in the warmer summer months.

　☐ October to April are the best times to visit, as the summers are often too hot and could cause heat strokes.

□ **Visiting Tips**

   □ Sources of water in the National Park are intermittent, so you'll need to pack all your own water in and out– at least a gallon a day per person.

   □ Water filling stations are available in the Visitor Centers and the Rincon District bike ramada.

   □ Take care on trails and watch for cacti, scorpions, and rattlesnakes.

   □ Regarding the saguaro cactus: it won't grow flowers until it turns 35 and it won't develop its first arm until it is 50-75 years-old.

   □ On a drive to the park, be sure to stop by the Arizona-Sonora Desert Museum near the Park's west entrance.

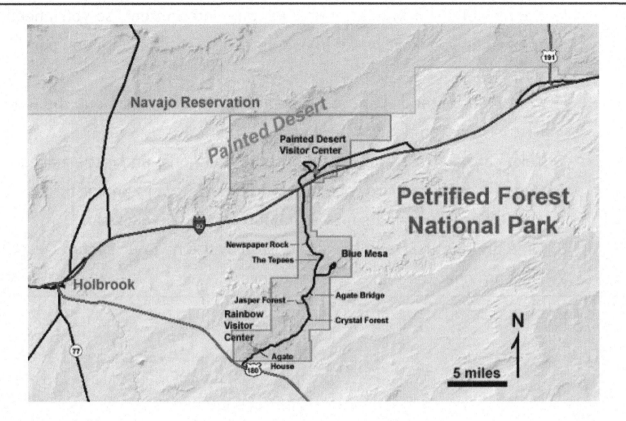

Overview

The Petrified Forest National Park is a place to view scenic wonders while learning about science and culture. The main draw for this park is the largest and most colorful concentrations of petrified wood in the world; it also features a number of historic structures, archeological sites, and fossils displays.

☐ **Visitor Centers / Hours**

    ☐ The park is open year-round except for Christmas.

    ☐ The park, including the visitor's centers, are open 7:00am-6:00pm.

    ☐ There are two visitor centers:

        ☐ Painted Desert Visitor Center

        ☐ Rainbow Forest Museum and Visitor Center

- **Fees**

  - Passes are good for 7 days.

    - $20 per vehicle
    - $15 per motorcycle
    - $10 per person

  - An annual pass is available for $40

- **Goods / Services**

  - Near the North Entrance, there is a convenience store, gas station, restaurant, and gift shop.
  - Near the South Entrance, there is a gift shop with limited snack options.

- **Pets**

  - Pets are allowed on any paved road or trail and all designated wilderness areas. However, only service animals are allowed in park buildings.
  - Pets must be on a leash no longer than six feet.

- **Camping**

  - Petrified National Forest doesn't have campground facilities.

- **Reservations / Permits**

  - Backcountry camping is available by permit. Permits can be obtained at the Visitor Centers for free.

- **Wildlife**

  - The wildlife includes coyotes, bobcats, porcupines, owls, falcons, lizards and turtles, and toads.
  - Common animals seen are migrating birds, rabbits, lizards, and snakes.

- **Weather**

  - Most of the park is semi-arid grassland. Temperatures can range from below freezing to well over 100 degrees Fahrenheit.
  - Snow is infrequent in the winter and thunderstorms are common in the summer.

- **When to Visit**

  - The park can be visited year-round, but come prepared for rather extreme temperatures if you are going to visit in the warmer summer months.

- **Visiting Tips**

  - The landscape is dry and no matter what time of the year you visit, you should make sure you pack enough water even for short day hikes.
  - Despite the dry climate, you are actually 5,800 feet above sea level, so you can easily feel winded in the thinner air.
  - Lastly, it can't be stressed enough: never take any samples of petrified wood from the park.

GRAND CANYON, ARIZONA

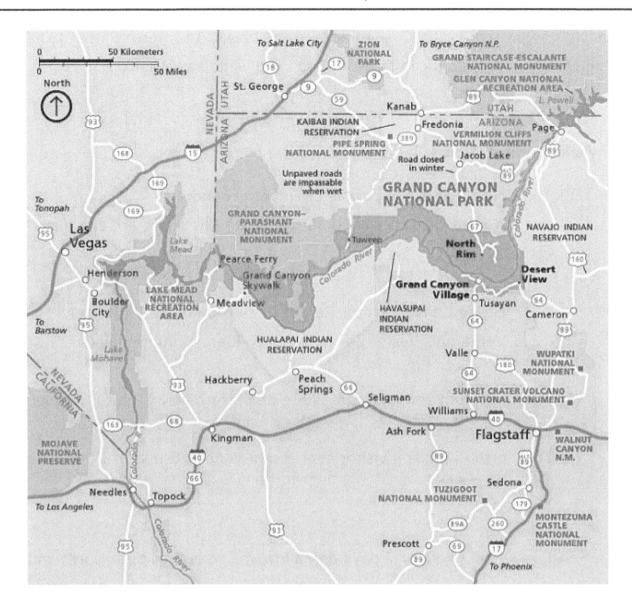

Overview

The Grand Canyon is something that really needs to be seen in order to be fully understood. The area is bursting with unique outdoor activities including hiking, donkey rides, and whitewater rafting. The park is one of the most visited in the world and has been a World Heritage Site since 1979, but it became a National Park in 1919.

The Grand Canyon National Park is divided into two public areas: the northern and southern rims. The South Rim is 7,000 feet above sea level and is the most accessible portion that visitors use to admire the views. The North Rim is 1,000 feet higher and is more difficult to get to, and the winter weather often closes access roads.

- **Visitor Centers / Hours**

  - The South Rim of the park is open year-round.
  - In the Grand Canyon Village on the South Rim there are two visitors centers:

    - Grand Canyon Visitor Center open 8:00am-6:00pm daily.
    - Verkamp's Visitor Center open 8:00am-8:00pm daily.

  - The North Rim and its facilities are open from May 15th to October 15th.
  - The North Rim has a visitor center that is open 8:00am-6:00pm daily.

- **Fees**

  - Passes are good for 7 days and allow you to access both North and South Rims.

    - $35 per vehicle
    - $30 per motorcycle
    - $20 per person

  - An annual pass is available for $70

- **Goods / Services**

  - The Grand Canyon Village on the South Rim features the following services:

    - Garage services for emergency repairs.
    - Groceries and general store.
    - Bank and ATM
    - Post office
    - Coin operated laundry and showers
    - Emergency medical care
    - Daycare
    - Kennel services

  - At the Desert View on the South Rim the following services are available:

    - Gasoline
    - Groceries and general store

  - The North Rim of the park features the following services:

    - Gasoline
    - Limited garage services
    - Coin operated laundry and showers
    - Post office
    - Camping supplies

- **Pets**

  - On the South Rim, pets on a leash no longer than six feet are allowed in the following areas:

- ☐ Trails above the rim
- ☐ Mather Campground
- ☐ Desert View Campground
- ☐ Trailer Village
- ☐ Developed areas

- ☐ On the North Rim, pets on a leash no longer than six feet are only allowed on the bridle trail.

☐ Camping

- ☐ There are four developed campgrounds in the Grand Canyon that allow drive-in camping.

  - ☐ The Mather Campground on the South Rim is open all year and requires reservations.
  - ☐ The North Rim Campground is open May 15 through October 31 and requires reservations.
  - ☐ Trailer Village in the only RV campground and is open all year.
  - ☐ Desert View Campground on the South Rim is open April 14 to mid-October and is a first come, first served.

☐ Reservations / Permits

- ☐ Reservations can be made through www.recreation.gov or through the park directly.

☐ Wildlife

- ☐ Nearly 500 species of animals are found in the national park area.
- ☐ Hundreds of bird species may be seen, including the endangered California Condor.

- The most common mammals in the park include coyotes, bats, mule deer, bighorn sheep, mountain lions, and elk.
- Use caution as scorpions are found at lower levels, and there are six species of rattlesnakes.

Weather

- The Grand Canyon presents a few extreme weather conditions.
- The South Rim is pleasant in the summer, but temperatures at the canyon floor can reach over 100 degrees Fahrenheit.
- Spring and fall are pleasant times, but the weather is unpredictable.

When to Visit

- The park can be visited year-round, but access to the North Rim can be limited in the winter.
- The best time to visit is early spring or late fall, since there are smaller crowds and less extreme weather.

Visiting Tips

- If traveling in the summer months, consider hiking at dawn or dusk to stay cool and hydrate appropriately.
- Most trails are shared, so if you encounter mules give them the right of way by stepping off the trail on the uphill side. Stand still and remain quiet until the mule is 50 feet past your position.
- The Ravens, rock squirrels, and deer mice are aggressive, so use animal-proof food storage containers for food, sunscreen, toothpaste, and lotion.

PART -2

WHAT TO SEE & DO IN A DAY TRIP

CHANNEL ISLANDS, CALIFORNIA

If you have just a day to visit the Channel Islands National Park, you should pick a single island to explore. If you are traveling in the spring through summer during whale season, then you can take an all-day whale-watching trip out of Venture or Santa Barbara Harbors.

Anacapa Island is the closest island to shore, at about 12 miles, which makes it the best island to visit if you are just making a day trip. A single hiking trail takes you two miles around the island to view wildflowers, birds, and sea mammals. If you have more time in the day or if hiking isn't your thing, you can also choose to kayak, swim, and snorkel at the Landing Cover, which is also a marine reserve.

It takes about an hour to get to the island by boat, and all boats take you to the east end of the island. There are no services there, so be sure to pack everything you need with you, including plenty of water and a picnic lunch if you plan to be on the island all day.

Start your trip at the small visitor center in one of the historic Coast Guard buildings at the landing area. It gives you a wide range of displays on the natural and cultural history of the islands.

Next, you can take a guided tour that occurs about every 30 minutes, or you can choose to hike the island and do other activities on your own.

Once you have climbed the stairway from the landing cove, you'll find the figure-eight-shaped trail system on the island is a relatively easy two-mile hike. The trail will take you over gentle slopes to stop at dramatic overlooks with breathtaking coastal views.

You'll also be able to see one of the last permanent lighthouses built on the West Coast. An entertainingly informative trip could even involve the use of an interpretive trail guide to learn about island resources as you hike.

If hiking isn't your thing, you have plenty of watersports options. While the island is a great place for swimming, diving, snorkeling, and kayaking, be aware there are no lifeguards on the island. This is why one should approach any water-related activities with responsibility and caution, particularly if there are younger children involved.

Most of Anacapa is built upon cliffs, so you can only access the water from the Landing Cove on the east end of the island via the boat dock. The underwater visibility here is very good and often features a lot of sea life since it is near a marine reserve. If you choose to kayak, head east towards Arch Rock or west towards Cathedral Cove to view wildlife, sea caves, and arches.

If you prefer to stay on land, then you still have several options for wildlife and wildflower-viewing on the island itself. Throughout the year, you'll be able to view a variety of seabirds including brown pelicans, cormorants, pigeon guillemots, and western gulls.

From Pinniped Point and Cathedral Cove, you'll be able to observe seals and sea lions. The best wildflower-viewing takes place in late winter and spring. The yellow coreopsis flowers peak in late January and March.

Other plants bloom in the summer including the gumplant, buckwheat, poppies and verbena. Frenchy's Cove on the west end of the island is available for tidepooling, which features mollusks, colorful corals, and a few hermit crabs.

DEATH VALLEY, CALIFORNIA

When visiting Death Valley National Park, there are several must-see things to do if you only have a day or less. Of course, consider taking a longer trek to fully enjoy all the park has to offer. Otherwise, let's look at what you can experience on a short trip. Just remember: if you are traveling in the warmer months, have plenty of water available.

Start your day trip at the Furnace Creek Visitor Center. From here, travel south on Highway 190 for about a mile and then turn right onto Badwater Road. Along with this path, your first stop is going to be Badwater Basin, which is the lowest elevation in North America, at 282 feet below sea level.

This salt flat gives you a unique experience and is only a short ¼ mile hike where you can view the polygon salt formations that Death Valley is known for. If you are traveling in the hot summer months, you can also view them from the comfort of the parking area.

Continuing on your drive, you'll next be able to drive through a rainbow of geology. Turn onto Artist's Drive– a one-way nine-mile drive that takes you through eroded and colorful desert hills. Along the way be sure to stop at Artist's Palette, and from the car or for a short walk, you can enjoy some very colorful views.

Lastly, drive to the most famous viewpoint in the park: Zabriskie Point. This viewpoint overlooks the golden-colored badlands. You can also choose to use this as a starting point to hike around the Badlands Loop. Connector trails allow you to visit Golden Canyon, Gower Gulch, and Red Cathedral based on the time you have to spend in the park.

JOSHUA TREE, CALIFORNIA

When you drive by Joshua Tree National Park for the first time, it may seem like a bleak and drab landscape, but there is a world of wonders waiting for just the right kind of perspective if one looks closely enough.

There is a variety of plants and animals to view, along with a number of geologic features and a rich cultural history to explore. There are plenty of options to take a look at for all types of interests and energy levels, all depending on how much time you intend to spend at this location.

For quick trips, you should start off at the visitor center to get information on the current conditions of the park. If you don't have a lot of time, you'll want to keep your sightseeing to the main park roads with their plentiful pullouts and exhibits.

Even if you are only staying a day or less, you will still have time to choose one of the 12 self-guiding nature trails to explore.

In the case of people who have more time at their disposal, take the additional 20-minute drive to Keys View. On a clear day, this visit allows you to view beyond the Salton Sea and all the way into Mexico.

If you are going to spend the entire day in the park, then you will be able to hike several of the nature trails. In order to understand the most from your visit, consider going on a ranger-led program.

You'll find listings for these at the visitor centers or on campground bulletin boards; you can also call ahead and reserve a spot on the more popular guided tours such as the Keys Ranch walking tour.

If you prefer to hike by yourself and enjoy the sounds of nature then plan an all-day hike into the backcountry.

If hiking isn't really your thing, you can consider doing some mountain bike riding. There are several dirt roads that offer a less crowded and safe option for mountain biking than the main paved roads would.

Another outdoor activity you can enjoy during your stay for the day is rock climbing. There are plenty of areas in the park to take advantage of a moderate rock climbing challenge.

SEQUOIA & KINGS, CALIFORNIA

While there are a lot of great outdoor activities to do in the combined Sequoia and Kings National Parks, it can be difficult to enjoy them both if you only have a day. The best way to truly bask in the marvels of each park is through a long drive and several stops at breathtaking vista points.

This way you can get a feel for the area, and you'll be able to plan your next long trip to the parks. Let's consider some of these scenic drives and vista points.

The first drive is on Generals Highway, which takes you from the Sequoia Park Entrance to Lodgepole. This drive is about an hour one way and takes you from the foothills into the sequoia groves. Since the road becomes narrow, there are some length advisories in place, and vehicles over 22 feet aren't advised.

From the Kaweah River to Hospital Rock, you'll wind up the rapidly-descending river through the Kaweah Canyon. Stop at Hospital Rock to see examples of Native American pictographs and mortars and immerse yourself in the history behind each item. Next, you'll come to Amphitheater Point. Here you'll be able to get a side view of Moro Rock, as well as the foothills up into the alpine peaks.

A third stop is at the Eleven Range Overlook. If you are here on a clear day, the views can extend to California's Coast Range across the San Joaquin Valley. Then there is Beetle Rock, which requires a short hike from the Giant Forest Museum. From here, you can see a flat expanse of granite with wide views of the surrounding area.

An extra location here would be Crescent Meadow– the location can be found after taking the side road to its end. If time permits, you can continue the drive up the Generals Highway from Lodgepole to Grant Grove. This portion takes you along mountain roads that stay at the same elevation and can take 45 minutes to an hour to complete. As you drive, a bridge carries you across the large Halstead Meadow.

On the north side, you'll find a small picnic area with a pit toilet that offers a great place to stop. If traveling in the spring, you may sometimes be able to see black bears in the meadow, so remember to approach situations involving wild animals with caution. Nonetheless, no matter what time of the year you travel, you'll be able to view beautiful wildflowers in this meadow.

Next, you'll arrive at the Redwood Mountain Overlook, which grants you a wide open view to the largest intact sequoia grove in the world.

The following stop is the Kings Canyon Overlook. Here you can look east into the vast wilderness that is Sequoia and Kings Canyon National Parks. If time permits, the last leg of this particular drive is Grant Grove to the Kings Canyon and Cedar Grove. This drive is 45 minutes to an hour and takes you into one of the deepest canyons in the United States.

The first destination in this incoming new drive is Junction View. From here you can see both the Middle and South Forks of Kings Canyon. Stopping at Yucca Point, you'll be able to look straight down into the junction of the Middle and South Forks of the Kings River.

When you're on Highway 180 between Yucca Point and Boyden Cave be sure to drive carefully. This section of road was blasted from the sheer walls of Kings Canyon. If possible, frequently pause to enjoy the natural, magnificent beauty of this water-carved canyon.

A worthwhile pit stop to thoroughly immerse yourself into is the Boyden Cavern. This marble cave is open in the summer for tours. You'll be able to notice thick layers of gray and white marble between strips of porous volcanic rock.

For those who are more used to staying outdoors instead of venturing into caves, you can take a five-minute walk to the impressive Grizzly Falls. This is an excellent, cool, and shady spot if you're visiting on a warm day.

Think of picnics, hikes, admiring wildflowers and local bird species, and any other activities surrounded by fresh air and the sweet scent of baking grass.

Shortly after, once you reach the Canyon View. From this pullout, you'll have an excellent oversight of the U-shaped Kings Canyon, where you can appreciate the glacial past of the parks.

In continuation, take the short walk toward Roaring River Falls. This small waterfall is quite powerful despite its size, as it comes through a narrow granite chute. Worry not when it comes to getting there since it is an easy, paved trail bound to suit any level of experience in hiking.

The last stop before the end of this trek takes place at Zumwalt Meadow. An effortless trail takes you to views of high granite walls, a lush meadow, and the breathtaking Kings River. An accessible boardwalk leads you to the meadow's edge or will allow you to continue on a 1.5-mile loop trail around the entire meadow.

Then you'll come to the road's end where you can have excellent views and access to river trails if you have time to hike one, in which case be sure to hike to Muir Rock.

LASSEN VOLCANIC, CALIFORNIA

There are many activities to do at Lassen Volcanic National Park fitting for each one of the four seasons. The best time to visit is in the summer months, so let's look at what you should plan to do while you take a day trip to this National Park in that season.

Start by taking a drive along the main park road and stopping at the many scenic vistas it has to offer. If you have time to spare, take a moment to go through one of the many popular hiking trails. A one-way trip along the main park road will take you about an hour without any stops and good weather.

Traveling the Sulphur Works gives you the easiest access to the active hydrothermal area. Take a stroll along the sidewalk that leads from the parking area to the mud pot and steaming vents of this natural wonder.

You should also make a mental note to visit Lake Helen at the base of Lassen Peak. At this elevation, the lake often has snow and ice, even into the mid-summer months. The views of the mountain peak from here are also breathtaking, and the picnic area offers a great place to stop for lunch.

Another trail to take if you have time is the Bumpass Hell Trail that takes you to the largest hydrothermal area of the park. This is a three-mile round-trip hike that takes you to a boardwalk where you can listen to the mud pots, watch steam escape from the Big Boiler fumarole and view the bubbling and boiling water pools.

If you are interested in the history of this location, take the accessible Devastated Area Interpretive Trail. This trail offers views of the destruction from the eruptions in 1914 and 1917 and offers several exhibits along the trail.

If you're traveling with family, consider taking the Mill Creek Falls Trail. This is a moderate 3.2-mile round-trip hike that guides you through the Red Fir Forest and takes you to the parks highest waterfall. This trail is often the first to have no snow and is located in the southwest area of the park.

If you are looking for more to do for the day other than driving or hiking, head to Manzanita Lake. Here you can take delight in a range of activities such as swimming, bird-watching, kayaking, and ranger-led programs.

For hiking in groups or as an individual, you can take the Manzanita Lake Trail starting at the Loomis Museum and continues for a 1.5 mile trip around the lake. The north end of the trail gives you beautiful views of the mountain peak as well as the surrounding area.

If you plan to visit in winter, there are a couple of activities you should definitely consider doing. Many people head to the steep slopes in the Southwest Area of the park near the Kohm Yah-mah-nee Visitor Center to partake in some sledding in the winter months. You will find a range of slopes to meet your specific group and conditions. Beware, since the icy snow creates very fast sledding conditions and there are a lot of trees and rocks in the area, so choose your sledding location carefully in order to prevent accidents.

Another popular winter activity is snowshoeing. There are free ranger-led snowshoe walks for those who are new to snowshoeing. When you venture out on your own, the Manzanita Lake Area and the snow-covered Park Highway Route provide gradual climbs with limited avalanche danger. For more difficult trails, consider the Southwest Area of the park.

PINNACLES, CALIFORNIA

Pinnacles National Park is a relatively small park with loads to see and do. It is possible to experience all of the park's trails in a few days, but if you only have a day or less to explore, then there are a few options that can help you enjoy every single nook of wonderful experiences the park has to offer.

One hike you can't miss while touring the park is the High Peaks Loop. This is a 9.3-mile loop, immersive trail that allows you to view the surrounding. You'll be able to explore the wild talus caves, walk among the park's volcanic spires, and climb over lichen-covered boulders and stairs chiseled into the rock to encounter sweeping views of wildflowers at the end of the road.

You may also be able to sight the endangered California condor if you are lucky enough. The entire trail has about 1,500 feet of elevation gain, and the highest point takes you 2,575 feet above sea level.

If you are not too interested in the lengthier types of hiking trails, there are some shorter options that still allow you to experience the park. Consider the Condor

Gulch Overlook. This moderate 2-mile hike has about 1,000 feet of elevation gain and takes you to a breathtaking view of the High Peaks without having to hike through them.

If you still have time and want to continue after reaching the overlook, then you can continue climbing uphill and connect with the High Peaks Trail.

Whether you only have a short time at the park or if you are looking to spend additional time, be sure to see the talus caves. You can access them along the easy Balconies Caves trail. It is a little over five miles and has minimal elevation gain.

Along the trail, you'll also be able to view all the habitats of the park, including a sunny stream-side to cave crawling. The last half mile of the trail takes you up a carved staircase. Be sure to pack a flashlight if hiking this trail.

REDWOOD, CALIFORNIA

There is plenty to see in the Redwood National Park. Known as the "Avenue of the Giants," this iconic area is often viewed from the 31-mile section of old Highway 101 that takes you through the Humboldt Redwoods State Park.

Let's look at what you can do to experience all the natural wonders of this gorgeous destination in a north to south trip through the park in a single day.

Start by discovering Howland Hill Road, a 10-mile scenic drive through the old-growth redwoods that follows Mill Creek. Take a walk to Stout Grove, a short half-mile hike through a river bottom grove of trees.

Next, stop to explore the Enderts Beach and Crescent Beach Overlook. Here you'll have beautiful views of the Pacific Ocean, and depending on the time of the year you travel, you may also be able to spot a gray whale. Take a one-mile walk to Enderts Beach, where you'll discover multi-colored tidepool creatures, so remember to travel during low tide times in order to witness all of the varieties of sea creatures in them.

Your next stop is at the Klamath River Overlook.

This is a great spot to watch the gray whale migration. You'll also be able to spot other marine mammals throughout the year and a range of seabirds. If you're up for it, take a hike down the ¼ mile steep trail to the lower overlook for even more breathtaking views.

If you have time, go for a side drive down Coastal Drive. This eight-mile road leads you past beautiful Pacific Ocean views, and you can stop to visit the World War II Radar Station and the High Bluff Overlook. If you bring binoculars, you can look at the large offshore rocks to view thousands of nesting seabirds.

Take the Newton B. Drury Scenic Parkway. This is far better than the traditional Avenue of the Giants. It is a 10-mile scenic drive that takes you through the ancient redwoods. Stop to venture forward in a ⅛ mile walk toward Big Tree, and you may even spot Roosevelt elk grazing in the prairie.

If you want a greater chance to spot Roosevelt elk, hop in your car and drive down Davison Road to Elk Meadow. You can also access Trillium Falls Trail– a 2.5-mile loop trail that takes you through ancient forests and features one of the few waterfalls in the park. This specific trailhead also offers picnic tables and restrooms, so it is a great place to stop for lunch.

Continue on Davison Road to the gray sands of Gold Bluffs Beach. Here you can even catch a glimpse of some remains from the mining era. An option for the plant and wildflower fanatic would be to hike Fern Canyon, which features 30-foot walls full of ferns.

Even if you travel in the summer and stick to foot bridges, you should expect to get your feet wet with either the water droplets in grass, rain, puddles, or mud.

You may also need to turn back to the parking area after a ¼ mile or so if there are large logjams.

End your trip at this national park by stopping at the Kuchel Visitor Center about a mile south of the town of Orick. This is the largest visitor center for the park and displays numerous exhibits and beach access.

YOSEMITE, CALIFORNIA

Yosemite is an enormous park and is about the size of the state of Rhode Island. Most people spend their time within the Yosemite Valley or about seven square miles. Within this area, there are 10 different hiking trails that provide breathtaking views at every turn.

We'll be talking more about Yosemite later, so, for now, we'll just look at the most important trails you'll want to take if you only have a day to spend at the park.

Perhaps the most popular and well-known hiking experience in Yosemite is the Mist Trail. This is a short, yet challenging trail that provides excellent views of two waterfalls that are over 900 feet tall when combined. It will also highlight access to the John Muir Trail, where you can view the popular sights of Nevada Fall, Liberty Cap, and Half Dome.

When you are hiking along the Mist Trail, you'll have a few side options depending on your time and hiking experience. At Happy Isles, in the eastern part of Yosemite Valley, the trail starts at 4,000 feet, and you climb about 1,000 feet to the top of Vernal Fall. You then continue another 1,900 feet up to the top of Nevada Fall.

While this doesn't seem like much, there is a lot of climbing involved, so be sure to plan your trip carefully. On the other hand, choosing the Mist Trail will take you to the top of Vernal Fall by a granite stairway of over 600 steps.

Another popular hike is Half Dome. Be prepared, though, since this is one of the longest and steepest day hikes in all of Yosemite. The entire trip is about a 14-mile round-trip and offers gains of nearly 5,000 feet. In order to get to the top of Half Dome, you need to make a nearly vertical climb aided by a set of cables.

When wet, this trek can be very hazardous. The view at the end is possibly the best in the park.

Just keep in mind that permits are required to hike Half Dome when the cables are up, and from Memorial Day weekend to Columbus Day, there is a lottery system in place to distribute summer permits.

CRATER LAKE, OREGON

Most people choose to visit Crater Lake in July, August, or September. This is when the majority of roads, trails, and facilities are open. May and June are the months when the park is transitioning from winter to summer.

I'm going to talk about taking a day trip in these months since it gives you plenty of options to do things or gives you an opportunity to view the entire park in a single day while experiencing all the seasons.

In May and June, you may experience anything from sunny skies to severe snowstorms, so you will need to pack and plan accordingly. In May, the average daily high is about 50 degrees Fahrenheit with an average monthly snowfall of 20 inches. At park headquarters, the average snow depth can sometimes be as high as six feet.

By June, the daily highs can average 69 degrees Fahrenheit. The average snowfall is down to 4 inches, but the average snow depth can still be two feet.

Do check the weather report before you go so you know what to expect and can plan your park activities accordingly.

Start your day with a drive to Rim Village that provides an overlook of the lake. On a clear day, you'll get breathtaking lake views of clear blue water surrounded by soft waves. Oftentimes, the road around Crater Lake to the North Entrance will still be closed due to snow. However, this doesn't limit the activities you can do.

A great way to explore the park in these months is by snowshoe. The Rim Village Gift Shop will rent you a pair for $16, and the Visitor Center can give you recommendations for where to go.

If you don't want to snowshoe, you should stick to Rim Drive. Sections of this road are likely plowed, but not yet open to cars. You can hike these sections and bask in the beauty of the park.

If you prefer to stay indoors and learn about the history behind several landmarks and natural monuments, head to the Steel Visitor Center at Park Headquarters and watch a 22-minute film on the past and present of the park.

The video is shown every half hour. Another great indoor opportunity is Crater Lake Lodge. Here you can view history exhibits, relax in the Great Hall, or listen to a ranger talk that is presented at 4pm and covers a range of topics.

Of course, you can simply photograph and play in the snow outside. The options are endless when visiting Crater Lake in May and June.

MOUNT RAINIER, WASHINGTON

Mount Rainier National Park has over 300 miles of trails to explore, so a short day hike is going to leave you with a lot of options. There aren't many easy trails in this park, so you'll need to make sure you're prepared and plan appropriately.

Let's look at some of the more popular trails you can take when planning a day hike at this location.

The best-known trail in the park is the Skyline Loop, taking you from Paradise up to Glacier Vista and Panorama Point. From these vantages, at the end of the trail, you can view the Nisqually Glacier and the dome of Mount Rainier along with the expansive Tatoosh Range to the south.

On a clear day, you may even be able to see Mount St. Helens.

Another popular hike in the park is Spray Park, which leads you to one of the most beautiful parklands in Mt. Rainier. A little detour will take you to Spray Falls, a 300-foot waterfall that drops down lava-rock cliffs.

Lastly, there is the Wonderland Trail. This 93-mile loop trail circles around the base of the volcano that mostly hugs the timberline and provides you great views of the ice-clad mountain from all sides.

It isn't possible to complete this entire hike on a day trip, but it will give you a great view of the mountain no matter how far you are able to hike.

NORTH CASCADES, WASHINGTON

Most of the hiking trails in North Cascades National Park are found along the North Cascades Scenic Highway or SR-20. You have plenty of day hiking opportunities if you are only visiting for a day, but let's discuss some of your best options so you can really enjoy the park.

Perhaps the best day hike is the Cascade Pass to Sahale Arm that is accessed off Cascade River Road. It is a moderate to strenuous hike that can be either a 7.5 to 12-mile round-trip depending on how far you choose to go. If you are able, it is best to take the longer route and go all the way to Sahale Glacier.

While on the trail, you'll experience 3,000 feet in elevation gain, so you should start your day early and take your time. Along the way, you'll come across a diverse variety of wildflowers and possibly even a bear, since they are regularly sighted in the trail.

However, if this trail isn't for you, there are plenty of other equally remarkable ones to experience. Some shorter and easier trails you can consider are the four-mile round trip Watson Lakes Trail, or the Boulder River Trail. Both of these offer absolutely amazing waterfall views after just a mile.

If you want something a little longer with more breathtaking sights, consider the 10.4-mile round-trip trail that takes you to the summit of Hannegan Peak. From here, you can enjoy panoramic landscapes such as the Cascade Range and Mount Baker.

A shorter option is Thunder Knob, which is a 3.6-mile hike with views of Diablo Lake and the surrounding mountains. This trail also allows you to take your dogs with you.

If you want something else to do besides hiking, consider boating on the nearby Ross Lake. This is especially popular in the summer because of the campsites along the shore with boat access. Just keep in mind that the winds can get gusty on the lake, so you should head out in the morning.

If you want to capture images of wildlife while in the park, you should head to the west bank of Willow Lake. This is just north of Ross Lake, and there have been many sightings of moose, coyotes, and gray wolves.

OLYMPIC, WASHINGTON

When visiting Olympic National Park, there is a lot to see and do. However, let's look at what places you can delve deeper into if only have a few hours to a whole day to spend there. Start your trip at the Olympic National Park Visitor Center in Port Angeles. Here you can view exhibits, watch an orientation film, and get guidance on how to make the most of your time at the park.

If you only have a few hours to burn, then you can consider the following options:

Take a 45-minute drive from Port Angeles to Hurricane Ridge. This will take you to the lowlands, where you'll encounter old growth forests of subalpine firs that give way to vast, open meadowlands. On a clear day, you'll enjoy breathtaking views of the Olympic Mountains and the Strait of Juan de Fuca.

Another option from Port Angeles is to drive about 30 minutes west to Lake Crescent. Here you can take a 12-mile hike along the shores of this lake carved by glaciers.

From Forks, you can take a 20-minute drive to Rialto Beach. Take a walk along the beach and chance seeing a bald eagle soaring overhead.

If you have a little more time and want to spend the entire day at the park, you'll be able to check out all of the major ecosystems in Olympic National Park: mountains, forest, and coast.

Again, taking a trip to Hurricane Ridge will take you about a mile in elevation, and here you'll find a visitor center and a vast number of nature trails. If you start early in the morning, you'll increase your likelihood of viewing wildlife as well as your chances of avoiding the larger crowds that gather later in the day.

From Hurricane Ridge, you can take a three-hour drive west to reach the Hoh Rain Forest. Here you can rest at a visitor center, go on walks over short nature trails, and eat a filling meal at the picnic area for your lunch.

Once you leave the Hoh Rain Forest, you can drive an hour and a half northwest to Rialto Beach and view the Pacific Ocean just in time for sunset.

GREAT BASIN, NEVADA

Caves, exhibits, challenging and also simple hikes, and wildlife. All of these can be found at the Great Basin National Park in the great state of Nevada. One could say it is a far more recreational trip than simply going to Las Vegas, for instance.

If you are not too sure of which places to visit at the park first, you could always stop in at a visitor center first to get recommendations on activities for your day. If you only have a half to a whole day consider the following activities.

If you only have half a day, there are four things you simply must do:

1. View the exhibits at both visitor centers.

2. Take a Lehman Caves Tour. For this, a park ranger will take you on a guided tour of the Lodge Room or Grand Palace sections of Lehman Caves.
3. Drive Wheeler Park Scenic Drive. 12 miles of unparalleled views of the valleys and mountain peaks.
4. Take a short hike along the Island Forest Trail. This ¼ mile trail is at the end of Wheeler Park Scenic Drive.

If you have an entire day to spend in the park, here are five things you should do:

1. Take the self-guided Mountain View Nature Trail. This trail starts beside the Lehman Caves Visitor Center and gives you the chance to experience a pinyon-juniper forest.
2. Another option while at the Lehman Caves Visitor Center is to attend a ranger program. Check the bulletin board for subjects that might interest you.
3. Take the time to enjoy your lunch at the secluded Pole Canyon Picnic Area off Baker Creek Road.
4. Take a hike up the Bristlecone Pine Trail, giving you a chance to see the oldest living trees in the world; it is a 2.8-mile round trip hike. You can also choose to head further up the trail to see the only glacier in the state of Nevada at the base of Wheeler Peak. Yes, you read that right. Glacier.
5. If you have plans to stay after sunset, take a moment to do some stargazing or participate in a ranger-led astronomy program. The Great Basin National Park features some of the darkest night skies in the United States, making it the perfect place to see shooting stars, planets, and the Milky Way glinting brightly over the desert.

SAGUARO, ARIZONA

The city of Tucson divided the Saguaro National Park into two districts: the western Tucson Mountain District and the eastern Rincon Mountain District. These districts are about an hour from each other.

The eastern portion is larger and has more mountains, while the western portion is lower and has a denser population of the saguaro cactus.

If you only have a day to spend here, there are more hiking trails in the east, and that is also the only area where backpacking is allowed; but the west is a better choice if you don't have a lot of time.

Let's look at what you can do in both districts.

WEST TUCSON MOUNTAIN DISTRICT

The best way to get an overall sense for the park is to drive the unpaved Bajada Loop. This 6-mile drive gives you great views of the foothills with plenty of stops for photo opportunities, picnic areas, and several hiking trailheads.

If you want to get out and hike while driving this loop, consider the Signal Hill Trail. This is an easy half-mile hike with 360-degree views of the area and the opportunity to observe many ancient petroglyphs. At the end of your hike, the shaded Ez-Kim-in-Zin picnic area is an excellent spot for lunch.

Another strenuous yet fantastic hiking opportunity in the western district is the Kings Canyon Trail. It takes you to the very top of the 4,687-foot Wasson Peak. The hike is a moderate round-trip climb of 6.5 miles and about 2,000 feet of elevation gain. Along with this hike, you'll see palo verde trees, prickly pear cactus, cholla, ocotillo, mesquite, mature saguaros, and petroglyphs.

EAST RINCON MOUNTAIN DISTRICT

To get a feel for the area, take an eight-mile drive along the Cactus Forest Loop. Here you'll enjoy wonderful views of the Rincon Mountains. There are plenty of hikes of varying distances and difficulties along this road if you want to get out and stretch your legs. One of the best options is the short one-mile Freeman Homestead Trail that firsthand introduces you to the saguaros the park is famous for.

If you want to learn about the wildlife in the area, consider taking the Desert Ecology Trail where you'll find interpretive signs for the plants and animals found in the Sonoran Desert. It is also an excellent trail with activities for kids if you are traveling with a family.

If you have a whole day and don't want to spend your time driving, consider hiking the Tanque Verde Ridge Trail. This 18-mile round-trip hike features 4,750 feet of vertical gain that occurs along a narrow, steep ridgeline while reaching the highest point on the ridge at 7,049 feet at the Tanque Verde Peak.

This trek isn't easy, and you should make sure you are prepared for it in terms of equipment and gear.

The hike will take you through six biotic zones of the area. Starting with cactus lowlands, pine forests, and mountainous vistas. Along the way, there are plenty of wildlife viewing opportunities including various species of reptiles and birds.

PETRIFIED FOREST, ARIZONA

Because Petrified Forest National Park isn't very big and doesn't have campgrounds for overnight stays, it is possible to see the majority of the park in a day if you stick to designated trails.

However, if you have time, you can stay in nearby towns then take several days to enjoy more of the off-trail options and other outdoor activities the park possesses. For a day trip, consider the following trails and see how many you can get done in that duration of time.

PAINTED DESERT RIM TRAIL

This trail is a one-mile round trip and can be reached from either Tawa Point or Kachina Point. It is an unpaved trail that takes you through rim woodland and includes many plants and animals as well as a breathtaking view of the Painted Desert.

PUERCO PUEBLO

This trail is a very short 0.3-mile loop trail. It can be accessed through the Puerco Pueblo parking area. This is a paved walk that guides you through the ruins of a 100-room pueblo that was once occupied by the ancestral Puebloan over 600 years ago. At the south end of the trail, you can view petroglyphs.

BLUE MESA

This one-mile loop trail is accessed via the Blue Mesa sun shelter. This trail alternates from pavement to gravel and descends from the mesa. It provides you with a unique hiking option among the badland hills filled with bluish bentonite clay and petrified wood of all shapes and sizes. You'll find a number of plant and animal fossils along the way.

CRYSTAL FOREST

This short 0.75-mile loop trail is accessed from the Crystal Forest parking area. This area is named for the beautiful rainbow-hued crystals often found in the center portions of petrified logs, and this trail is your best chance to view petrified wood deposits.

As stunning as the crystals and the petrified wood are, it is extremely important to not pick up any pieces and to leave the section exactly as it was when you arrived to it. If you see anything out of the ordinary, make sure to report any observances to the park staff.

GIANT LOGS

This is another short 0.4-mile loop that is found behind the Rainbow Forest Museum. Here you'll find some of the largest and most colorful petrified wood samples in the park. In fact, the sample at the top of the trail is nearly ten feet wide at the base.

The paved trail has several areas of stairs that may not be accessible by all people, but the rest of the open zones are equally as worthwhile to explore and appreciate at a geological level.

LONG LOGS

This particular path can be combined with the Giant Logs Trail. The Long Logs Trail is a 1.6-mile loop that starts from the Rainbow Forest Museum parking area. You can explore an ancient log jam at the base of the powder-gray badlands.

The first half mile of the trail is paved, but it turns narrow and rough the deeper one gets into it.

AGATE HOUSE

This is the longest trail in the park at a two-mile round-trip hike. It is also accessed from the Rainbow Forest Museum parking area, conveniently enough. This small pueblo was believed to be occupied for a short time about 700 years ago.

The Agate House is an eight-room home that was accessed from the ceiling. The first half-mile of the trail is paved, but then becomes rougher later in the hike.

If you only have a day to visit the Grand Canyon, you're missing a lot. But there are still several wonderful day hikes you can take, worry not. The most important thing to keep in mind is that you can't hike from the rim to the river and back in a single day, especially if you are visiting in the months of May to September.

We'll look into longer options at the Grand Canyon later, but for now, let's look at the options available to day hikers.

SOUTH RIM DAY HIKES

RIM TRAIL

This trail extends from the village area to Hermits Rest. Start from any viewpoint in the village or along Hermit Road. The Rim Trail allows you to walk and enjoy quiet views of the inner canyon. This is a very easy day hike that nearly anyone can make.

BRIGHT ANGEL TRAIL

This is a steep trail that starts just west of Bright Angel Lodge and provides day hikes of up to 12 miles of a round-trip. There is some shade on this hike, but it is still recommended to bring sunscreen or a head cover like a bandanna or a cap, just for those with sensitive skin. If traveling in the early spring or winter portions, watch out, as this trail can get icy.

SOUTH KAIBAB TRAIL

The South Kaibab Trail is another steep one that starts south of Yaki Point on Yaki Point Road. You can get to the trailhead by shuttle bus along the Kaibab Trail Route. It provides six-mile, round-trip day hikes, allowing you to appreciate wide landscape views Be aware, as there is little shade on this hike and the temperatures can and will get on the higher end of the scale.

Again, if traveling in the early spring or winter, the upper portion of the trail can be icy, so come prepared with the correct equipment such as hiking boots.

HERMIT TRAIL

This is the third consecutive steep trail that takes you to Santa Maria Spring. The hike is a five-mile round-trip, and you can also take it a little farther to Dripping Springs, which is a 7-mile round-trip. The trail conditions are a little rougher and strenuous than the earlier hikes we've mentioned, as it is on rugged terrain with little to no paved road support. The trailhead is 500 feet west of Hermit's Rest.

Now, it is recommended that only experienced desert hikers take this trail, as it is not an easy type of experience to go on.

GRANDVIEW TRAIL

If you are searching for an even steeper trail that takes hikers to Coconino Saddle, this is the option for you. It is only a 2.2-mile round-trip, but do not be fooled by the length. You can choose a longer round-trip hike of 6.4 miles to Horseshoe Mesa. Trail conditions are very tough and require caution when hiking.

Some of the dangers involve overexertion, dehydration due to the high temperatures in the summer, flash flooding in the rain season, and possible poisonous reptiles along your path such as rattlesnakes.

It starts on the canyon side of the retaining wall at Grandview Point on Desert View Drive about 12 miles east of the village. This hike is only recommended for experienced desert hikers.

NORTH RIM DAY HIKES

BRIGHT ANGEL POINT TRAIL

This short trail is a half-mile round-trip and only takes about 30 minutes. It is a paved trail with beautiful views of the canyon. The trail starts at the log shelter in the parking area by the visitor center.

You can also get a self-guided nature pamphlet for this trail since cell phone service is very spotty and it is always a good idea to carry a physical map with you in case of any technical difficulties along the way.

TRANSEPT TRAIL

This is a three-mile round-trip trail that takes about an hour and a half to hike. It takes you along the canyon rim from the Grand Canyon Lodge to the North Rim Campground. Some of the perks throughout this route involve gorgeous landscape views and tons of wildflowers.

Not to mention, the level of difficulty is actually pretty mild, but do not forget your water bottles and sunscreen, or any other pieces of equipment that could come in handy when one least expects it.

BRIDLE TRAIL

This is a 1.2-mile, one-way hike. It follows the road as it connects the Grand Canyon Lodge to the North Kaibab Trailhead. This is a hard-packed trail that permits bicycles and pets on a leash. There might occasionally be horses allowed depending on overnight permit limitations from the park itself.

Overall, it is a relatively easygoing option for the beginner hiker.

NORTH KAIBAB TRAIL

The distance and hiking times on this trail will vary. It is the only maintained trail into the canyon from the North Rim. The short part of the hike is a 1.5-mile round-trip to the Coconino Overlook. The longer option is a 4-mile round-trip to the Supai Tunnel. Either option will allow you to experience the natural beauty and size of the Grand Canyon.

Other options from this trail are the strenuous Roaring Springs that will often take seven to eight hours to hike. It is best to start this route before 7am. Roaring Springs is 3,050 feet below the canyon rim and is a 9.4-mile round-trip hike that will most likely take you all day.

It is not recommended you try to hike beyond Roaring Springs in a single day, but rather to rest between destinations and plan out your route very well on the map beforehand. For this, you can acquire an overnight camping permit from the park and set up a tent in one of the pre-established camping grounds.

KEN PATRICK TRAIL

This is a 10-mile one-way hike lasting about six hours. It takes you through forests and along the rim from Point Imperial to the North Kaibab Trail parking area.

UNCLE JIM TRAIL

Here goes a 5-mile round-trip hike that takes about three hours to complete. It takes you through forests to a point overlooking the canyon and the switchbacks of the North Kaibab Trail. It starts at the North Kaibab Trail parking lot. Be advised, as this trail is also used by mules. So, remember to give them the right of way and waiting until the road is clear.

WIDFORSS TRAIL

Another option is a 10-mile round-trip hike of about six hours. It blends both canyon and forest scenery, so the contrast makes for one very entertaining, immersive experience. Even a short walk on this trail is very enjoyable.

You take a dirt road ¼ mile south of Cape Royal Road for a mile before getting to the Widforss Trail parking area. You can find a self-guiding brochure at the trailhead.

CAPE ROYAL TRAIL

This is a short 0.6-mile round-trip hike that only takes about 30 minutes at a medium-slow pace. It is an easy hlke on a flat and paved trail with excellent views of the canyon as well as Angels Window and the foaming Colorado River. There are markers along the way that tell you about the natural history of the area. The trail starts from the southeast side of the Cape Royal parking area.

CLIFF SPRINGS TRAIL

This short one-mile round trip trail takes about an hour. It takes you down a lush forest ravine and ends under a large overhang. The trail starts across from the small pull-out on a curve about 0.3 miles from Cape Royal.

ROOSEVELT POINT TRAIL

This an even shorter 0.2-mile trail that takes about 20 minutes. However, this trail is great for those who want to relax and enjoy the canyon since it offers several bench options and takes you through secluded woodland covered in wildflowers and various types of nesting birds.

PART – 3

14-DAY PARK HOPPER TRAVEL PLANS

2-WEEK TRIP ITINERARIES

If you have two weeks to vacation and want to take an in-depth trip of the National Parks, there are some things you need to see. I'm going to give you two sets of two-week trip itineraries to offer you an idea of how you can spend a wonderful 14 days enjoying the beauty and outdoors at our National Parks.

ITINERARY #1: SOUTHERN CALIFORNIA

CHANNEL ISLANDS, JOSHUA TREE, DEATH VALLEY, SEQUOIA & KINGS, YOSEMITE, PINNACLES

It may seem like a lot, but with close driving time, it is possible to visit all of the above national parks in southern California. Spend two days at each park and have more time to see the important sites or adjust your plan as you like and focus your attention on one park.

CHANNEL ISLANDS

Start your two weeks with a relaxing ocean stay at the Channel Islands National Park. If you are going to have a quick overnight stay at this National Park, your best option is to choose Santa Cruz Island. It is the biggest of the five islands– as well as the easiest to get to– so you'll have plenty to do to keep you busy for two days in a row.

The weather on this island is the best, always reaching a warm and humid feeling without being overwhelming. Just make sure you plan in advance since there are no services on the island.

As with all of the islands at this National Park, you want to plan and reserve your transportation first before getting your campsite reservations. Island Packers is responsible for year-round travel to the island, and it typically takes about an hour to get there. Transportation drops you to either Scorpion Anchorage or Prisoners Harbor. It is best to get off at Scorpion Anchorage, speaking from experience.

In the Scorpion Anchorage area, you will find the Channel Islands Adventure Company. They are an authorized kayak guide and outfitting concession. Here you can plan your sea kayak tours, purchase limited convenience items (no food), rent snorkel equipment, or plan a guided snorkel tour. There are no other services in the area, so you will need to bring all your own food and supplies. There are also no public phones.

Begin your stay at the visitor center in the historic Scorpion Ranch House. At this location, you can find an orientation area that will help you plan your stay while also viewing a number of interactive exhibits on the biodiversity, cultural history, and resources of the island.

There is primitive camping available at the Scorpion Ranch Campground. There are 31 sites, and they cost $15 per night. Reservations are required. The campsites come equipped with water, picnic tables, food storage boxes, and pit toilets. Shade is available as well. It takes you a half mile to hike to the campsites from the landing.

Of all the islands, this one has the most family-friendly campground. There is backcountry camping available year-round at the Del Norte campsite near Prisoners Harbor.

Your biggest activity on this island is going to be hiking. There are 15 hiking trails and roads that traverse the eastern part of Santa Cruz Island. All of these trails range from less than a mile to 18 miles long. They also vary from maintained and relatively flat to unmaintained and rugged mountain paths.

No hiking is allowed beyond the national park boundary marked by a fence line between Prisoners Harbor and Valley Anchorage.

Most of the trails on the island have great views and start from the Scorpion Ranch Campground. The most popular is the two-mile hike from Scorpion Ranch Campground to Cavern Point.

This is a wonderful option for those who want to watch whales. A longer option is the five-mile Potato Harbor hike. There are also three trails from Smugglers Cove that are a short two, three and four miles, but they are strenuous hikes. The backcountry trails in Prisoners Harbor are all strenuous, as a matter of fact. The short half mile Prisoners Harbor Trail gives you a good overview of the historic area.

Another option on this island aside from hiking is the numerous watersports of the area. Scorpion Beach offers mixed sand and cobblestone with lots of opportunities for swimming, diving, snorkeling, and kayaking. You will have easy beach access from your campground, along with clear ocean waters with extensive kelp forests. For kayakers, there are also beautiful shoreline sea caves to explore. However, keep in mind that there are no lifeguards on duty at the island, so swim responsibly.

When it comes to diving and snorkeling, the easiest kelp bed access are the ones near the pier and those at the eastern end of the bay. You can also access the beach from Prisoners Harbor by hiking to Smugglers Cove, but the snorkeling here isn't as good. Kayak east towards Scorpion Rock and west towards Cavern Point, where you will have excellent wildlife-viewing opportunities and many sea caves.

There are also several locations on Santa Cruz Island that offer surfing options. The north shore is best in winter and spring when the northwest swells arrive. The south shore is best in the summer and fall when there are south swells. Keep in mind that all surf spots are remote and often need to be accessed by boat, since hiking the distance can be rugged.

Lastly, there are diverse wildlife and wildflower-viewings on Santa Cruz Island. Throughout the year, you can see a variety of seabirds, especially in the Scorpion Rock area. Most birders travel to the island in order to catch a glimpse of the endemic island scrub-jay, which is only found on Santa Cruz. The best place to glimpse these birds in action is at Prisoners Harbor.

The ranch and campground area of Scorpion Anchorage is the ultimate location to see island foxes. Just keep in mind that it is illegal to directly or indirectly feed the animals. Aside from causing health issues for the wildlife, it also could lead to dangerous situations where larger species approach you, so it is best to let these creatures find their food in their own habitat.

If there is a year of normal rainfall, wildflowers are best viewed in the late winter and spring months. There are also some plants such as the gumplant, buckwheat, poppies, and verbena that bloom into the summer months. Scorpion Anchorage and Prisoners Harbor also offer limited tidepooling options. The best tidepooling is seen at Smugglers Cove and includes all sorts of fun little mollusks and crustaceans.

DEATH VALLEY

After your stay at the Channel Islands, take a drive to Death Valley National Park for quite the contrast in climate and terrain. There are only a few constructed trails in this park, but with the desolate landscape you can often go off trail and enjoy the rugged, desertic nature around you from anywhere. Many of the hiking routes you choose in this park are cross-country, up canyons, or along ridges.

November through March are the best times to hike in the Death Valley. Summer temperatures can be very dangerous, especially at lower elevations, considering how during the month of May temperatures can reach an average high of 108.1 degrees Fahrenheit.

Needless to say, even in the autumn and spring, the heat can be unbearable for some people.

It is best to save morning low elevation hikes for cooler days in the winter. In the summer, the high peaks can offer an escape from the heat, but they can be covered with snow in the spring and winter. If you plan to climb the peaks in the winter, then you need to be properly equipped with winter clothing and winter climbing gear.

As the name suggests, since Death Valley has a dry climate, you will need to drink more water when visiting here than in other places– even if you are traveling during the cooler winter months. Carry adequate amounts of water with you at all times. In the winter, a short day hike would require at least two liters of water, while a longer hike in the warm season will require a gallon or more.

Springs are rare in the park and shouldn't be considered a reliable source of water. In addition, you should boil or treat any water sources before drinking if you do happen to come across one. Consider the following list of hikes available to you while staying at Death Valley National Park.

EASY HIKES

- ☐ Harmony Borax Works - 0.4 mile
- ☐ Salt Creek Interpretive Trail - 0.5 mile
- ☐ Badwater Salt Flat - 1 mile
- ☐ Natural Bridge - 1 mile
- ☐ Mesquite Flat Sand Dunes - 2 miles

MODERATE HIKES

- ☐ Ubehebe Crater Loop - 1.5 miles
- ☐ Darwin Falls - 2 miles
- ☐ Badlands Loop - 2.7 miles
- ☐ Golden Canyon - 3 miles

- ☐ Desolation Canyon - 3.6 miles
- ☐ Mosaic Canyon - 4 miles
- ☐ Willow Canyon - 4.2 miles
- ☐ Gower Gulch Loop - 4.3 miles
- ☐ Sidewinder Canyon - 5 miles
- ☐ Fall Canyon - 6 miles
- ☐ Dante's Ridge - 8 miles

DIFFICULT HIKES

- ☐ Panamint Dunes - 7 miles
- ☐ Little Bridge Canyon - 7 miles
- ☐ Corkscrew Peak - 8 miles
- ☐ Wildrose Peak - 8.4 miles
- ☐ Telescope Peak - 14 miles

If you have time while staying at the park, consider taking a special paleontology hike. These hikes take you to remote areas of the park that are often closed to the public and take place on selected dates during the winter and spring months. If you choose to take part in a paleontology hike, be prepared for an all-day, seven-mile round-trip that has about 1,500 feet of elevation gain along the rugged and uneven, searing terrain.

This kind of hike is considered moderately strenuous and isn't recommended for anyone with mobility and/or breathing issues, or those who are younger than ten years old. It is very suggested that people regularly hike at least four miles on uneven terrain in the weeks before as training to prepare them for the Death Valley's conditions.

Training and age limits aside, the paleontology hikes often take you into dramatic canyons with high cliff walls that open into multi-colored basins. You'll learn about stories dating back millions of years when life first appeared in Death Valley and how the ocean carved its way through the stone while leaving marine deposits behind. You will get a chance to view fossilized tracks from birds, horses, camels, and mastodon-like animals.

Although the hikes are limited to fifteen people, lottery entries are accepted during the sign-up period, and a single person can enter up to four people. There is no fee for the guided hike itself, but donations are allowed to help maintain and support the program which is offered through the Death Valley Natural History Association.

JOSHUA TREE

From Death Valley, you can travel to another desert landscape at Joshua Tree National Park. There is much more to this park than you may think when first looking at it and it is well worth at least an overnight stay. The park has nine established campgrounds, several hiking trails that range in distance but all have a great view of the park and plenty of granite climbing.

In fact, when you stay overnight, you might want to spend some time stargazing at one of the best places in Southern California to view the glimmering night sky.

The best way to experience the park is by camping there and taking at least two days to explore the peaks, mines, and wildlife. Some challenges to consider involve climbing all ten peaks in the park or hiking to all five of the fan palm oases. There are two main reasons why people come to this park: hiking or climbing.

For now, let's focus on the hiking options available during your stay.
The Hidden Valley Loop is a one-mile hike that is the most popular trail in the park. This scenic route takes you around gigantic boulders and gives you an

opportunity to watch some climbers in action. It is also a unique hike because it has a microhabitat where you can see all the plants found throughout the park including the Joshua Tree, pinyon, juniper, oak, mesquite, yucca, and several types of cacti.

A top nature walk in the park is the Cholla Cactus Garden hike. It is a very short 0.25-mile hike but it allows you to see a dense concentration of cholla cacti. This cactus has been nicknamed "teddy bear" because the way the hundreds of spines are distributed give it an almost fluffy appearance, but you still don't want to touch it.

Also, be particularly careful around any type of cholla cacti, since quite a few of them attack by jumping at whoever is nearby and lodging their spines on clothes and skin. If you do happen to get attacked by a cactus, the best way to remove the spines is by using a hair comb.

If you want a longer hike with a little more difficulty, you should consider the Lost Horse Mine and Mountain Trail that is 4 miles. This hike takes you out to the historic Lost Horse Mine where gold and silver was mined between 1894 and 1931.

Another long hike to take in mind is the seven-mile Lost Palms Oasis where you can view beautiful palm trees and pools of water as well as plenty of bighorn sheep. Depending on the season, the amount of water will vary, as it sometimes evaporates in the hotter months and leaves a thin layer of mud instead of an actual pool.

For a steeper climb, consider the three-mile Mastodon Peak Trail that takes you to the often passed up Cottonwood Spring area. Here you can enjoy unparalleled views of the Eagles Mountains and the Salton Sea. This mountain has an elevation of 3,371 feet, so the trek is strenuous, but takes you through the desert section of the park and gives you quite a different view from most hikes.

It also passes by Mastodon Mine, which was still operational until 1971. Before or after you reach the peak, you could take some time to enjoy the Cottonwood Spring Oasis.

One secret area of the park that you should make sure to explore is Indian Cove. You can only get to this specific location from Indian Cove Road, which is seven miles west of the town of Twentynine Palms. The Indian Cove Nature Trail is a half-mile long and guides you through flowery desert willows and desert almonds. When hiking in the spring and early fall, you'll also spot a desert tortoise or two.

If you are looking for a full-day hike, there are few routes better than the 6.5-mile long Maze Loop Trail. The name comes from the mini-slot canyons you hike along the way. You'll see examples of Joshua Trees as well as prickly pear cactus and spring wildflowers. You'll also spot plenty of desert horned lizards and chuckwalla lizards.

If you aren't in the mood to hike or simply want a day to relax after all the hiking you've done at the Channel Islands and Death Valley, you can always go on a drive around the park and stopping at the lookouts and rock formations such as Skull Rock.

The park offers an 18-mile Geology Motor Tour that features 16 stops along the way at some of the most fascinating geological spots in the park. The first few miles can be accessed by most vehicles, but you may need a 4WD to access the rest of the trail.

Lastly, make sure you stay overnight at least one night. This gives you a chance to view some of the best stargazing in Southern California, as you know. If you travel in the winter, it is often completely dark by 5:00pm so you'll have plenty of time to view the stars at a comfortable temperature before going off to bed.

In the winter you'll be able to glimpse constellations such as Orion, Sirius, Gemini, and Taurus. In the summer on moonless nights you have excellent views of the Milky Way. It is also an amazing place to view the Perseid Meteor Shower in mid-August.

SEQUOIA AND KINGS

The main reason people visit Sequoia and Kings National Parks is for the giant sequoia trees, but there are over 800 miles of beautiful trails to hike while visiting. You certainly want to at least spend a couple of days here. After you've spent time in the dry climates of Death Valley and Joshua Tree, this is a nice break with some milder and cooler weather.

The most important part of any visit to these parks is to visit a giant sequoia grove. There are several options for groves to visit.

The most popular is the Giant Forest Grove. This is set on a rolling plateau in Sequoia National Park between the Marble and Middle Forks of the Kaweah River. It is one of the largest unlogged sequoia groves. It is also home to the largest living sequoia tree, the approximately 2,000-year-old General Sherman Tree, standing at 84 meters, or 275.59 feet tall.

Within this grove, there is a number of hiking trails that can range from short hour hikes to half-day explorations. You can also learn about the natural and cultural history of the area by viewing the surrounding historic structures. For a challenging hike, climb Moro Rock. If you aren't open to hiking, you can visit the Giant Forest Museum and explore the area by car.

The best example in Kings National Park is the Grant Grove. You can access this from a short spur road off Highway 180 and is just 1.5 miles from the Kings Canyon Visitor Center. Within a 90-acre area, you'll find a high percentage of mature sequoia trees. A ⅓ mile paved loop takes you to the General Grant Tree. Other trails in the area lead you to meadows and wilderness-viewing areas.

Another large grove is the Redwood Mountain Grove. Here you'll find a spectacular example of old growth sequoias as well as a diversity of other plants and fungi that grow in the forest. If you are visiting in the spring, you'll also see a mix of wildflowers on the ridge trail near Redwood Creek. This is the largest grove in terms of total area and contains more mature sequoias than any other grove.

If you want a little more privacy and seclusion, consider the Muir Grove in Sequoia National Park. This is a mid-sized grove that is a two-mile hike from Generals Highway and is far less visited than other groves. The hike to this grove and beyond is a great day-exploration option.

Lastly, there is the Atwell and East Fork Groves that are found on the north and south slopes of the East Fork of the Kaweah River. You need to drive about 19 miles up the Mineral King Road off Highway 198 to access these groves. Both of these are on steep slopes, so it isn't an easy hike. The groves are also accessible from the Atwell Mill Campground if you want to stay in the area.

Once you've visited a few of the sequoia groves, there are still plenty of other hikes to enjoy. A great day hike to take is the Middle Fork Trail. This trail is a fantastic option since it allows you to go as far into the backcountry as you want. Most choose to stop and turn around at the three-mile mark when it reaches the Panther Creek Falls.

A side trail from this is the Marble Falls Trail. This 3.9-mile hike is a little more challenging but also features a beautiful waterfall. Another option is the easy Tokopah Falls hike that starts from the Lodgepole Campground.

For a great experience while at Kings National Park, you should visit Cedar Grove. This area is surrounded by granite cliffs, meadows, and the Kings River. There are several great hiking options here, but most are moderate to strenuous. The shortest and easiest of these hikes is the Zumwalt Meadow Trail at 1.5 miles in length.

A more challenging hike is the Cedar Grove Overlook Trail that is 5 miles with 1,200 feet of elevation gain and switchbacks that take you up the forested ridge. Lastly, there is the Lookout Peak Hike that takes you on a 13-mile round-trip hike to the 4,000-foot summit.

YOSEMITE

Yosemite National Park is a huge park and a popular tourist destination. You could easily spend days at this natural landmark and still not cover all there is to see. As one of the top ten National Parks in the United States, we'll look at this in greater detail shortly.

But for now, let's assume you are spending at least a couple of nights here while embarking on a two-week trip through the southern California national parks. Let's focus on a little-known part of the park and something that would be a unique experience for a short stay.

The area of Wawona wasn't added to the Yosemite National Park until 1932. This is a hidden area of Yosemite home to a mid-elevation basin and has many natural features. Originally, this territory belonged to the Native Americans but later was a settlement for those traveling to the Yosemite Valley in the late 19th century.

You can drive to Wawona year-round, although tire chains may be needed from October to April due to the thin layer of ice and snow that may appear. There is also a gas station available year-round.

From here, there are numerous activities, and it places you close to the main hub of Yosemite Valley without having to get into the large crowds of the touristic areas of Yosemite. If you are traveling from May to October, you should visit the Wawona Visitor Center at Hill's Studio.

Near the location, you will be able to find the Pioneer Yosemite History Center, which is open all year. Here, you can visit historic buildings from Yosemite's past including a covered bridge and horse-drawn wagons. Many of the buildings were moved to Wawona in the 50s and 60s. In the summer months, stage rides are available, and some buildings are open for you to explore or view demonstrations.

If you want to go outside, you should visit Chilnualna Falls, which reaches a peak flow in May. This waterfall consists of five cascades that slide through and over large granite formations just above the Wawona area. This trail is strenuous, and you can view the cascades at many points along the hike as well as views overlooking Wawona.

You are also near to the famous Mariposa Grove of giant sequoias where you can catch a glimpse of over 500 mature giant sequoias, just in case you didn't see enough of these when you were at Sequoia and Kings National Parks.

If you are only going to be there for a few days, you want to maximize your time. To do this, consider taking a year-round bus tour offered by Yosemite Hospitality. All of these tours start within Yosemite Valley and can give you a range of experiences. Check out some of your options:

The Valley Floor Tour takes you on a two-hour trip to Yosemite Valley and operates all year. From April through October, it is an open-air tram tour depending on the weather. From October through March it is a bus tour.

The four-hour long Glacier Point Tour walks you to Glacier Point and back. This tour operates when Glacier Point Road is open, which is often from late May until November based on weather conditions.

The Grand Tour is an all-day tour of about eight hours that takes you through Yosemite Valley, Glacier Point, and the Mariposa Grove of Giant Sequoias. This tour is available during late spring through summer of May to September, depending on the climate.

Lastly, there is the Tuolumne Meadows Tour that is an all-day tour which takes you to Tuolumne Meadows and back. The tour operates from July until early September, weather permitting, as always.

PINNACLES

End your two-week trip at Pinnacles National Park, where you'll experience over 30 miles of trails that bring the beauty of the park up close and personal for you. The hikes can range from flat ground with grasslands to uphill climbs in talus caves, to the rocky spires the Pinnacles are known for.

If it is your first visit to the park, be sure to stop by the Pinnacles Visitor Center to get some ideas on what to do first. Another option is to stay a night or two at the Pinnacles Campground and take a few of the various hikes that originate from this location.

The first one takes you from the Pinnacles Visitor Center to the Bear Gulch Day Use Area. This is a 2.3-mile, one-way hike lasting about an hour and a half. It is a moderate level of difficulty that follows Chalone and Bear Creeks.

Another option is the longer 6.5-mile round-trip trail that will have you travel from the Pinnacles Visitor Center to the South Wilderness Trail. This unmaintained trail of a hike will take you about three to four hours and is moderate in nature.

It covers the boundary of the park and along the way passes through a grove of valley oaks. It is a great trail option for those who want to observe birds and other sorts of wildlife.

Your last option is to hike from Pinnacles Visitor Center to Balconies Cave. This is a 9.4-mile round-trip trail that takes about four to six hours. It is a moderate hike that follows Chalone Creek. On your way back you can cross over the cave on the Balconies Cliffs Trail to view some of the largest rock formations in the park.

Be sure to pack a flashlight and extra batteries for when you enter the cave.

ITINERARY #2: WASHINGTON

MOUNT RAINIER, OLYMPIC, NORTH CASCADES

Another excellent two-week vacation option is to visit all the National Parks in Washington. Start in the south at Mount Rainier, then head west for the Olympic National Park, and end in the north at North Cascades. Determine how many days you want to spend at each park in order to immerse yourself in the surrounding landscapes.

MOUNT RAINIER

Mount Rainier has five developed areas that are worth exploring. If you have a few days to spend, you can easily choose any of these areas, but the one with the most unique and wide range of things to see is the Longmire District. Let's consider what you can see and do while staying in this developed area for a few days.

Mount Rainier was established as a National Park in 1899, and at that time, Longmire became the park headquarters. Previously, the site was James Longmire's homestead along with lodging and a mineral springs resort. While the park headquarters are no longer here, the original building still houses a museum that showcases its early days.

Across from the museum is the newer Longmire Administration Building that was completed in 1930 and still houses the Longmire Wilderness Information Center. Longmire is now a national historic district. It is located in the southwest corner of the park about 6.5 miles east of the Nisqually Entrance.

This area offers you two lodging options based on your taste and the experience you want to have. You can choose to stay at the National Park Inn which features a hotel, restaurant and gift shop that is typically open all year. The other option is to camp at the Cougar Rock Campground and Picnic Area about 2 miles east, which is typically open from late May to early October.

From either area, you can drive to several scenic areas with short hikes if you want to take it easy during your stay. Let's look at some of these areas:

Westside Road starts about one mile east of the Nisqually Entrance. The road is closed to vehicles beyond the gate but is still open for biking and walking.

Christine Falls is located about four miles east of Longmire, and after a short walk from the pullout, you can enjoy a classic view of the falls from a rustic stone bridge. Parking is limited here, and you don't want to stop or park on the bridge.

Glacier Bridge is five miles from Longmire as you head towards the developed area of Paradise. When crossing the bridge, you can get up to the valley and admire the Nisqually Glacier.

Ricksecker Point Road is a one-way road that starts six miles east of Longmire and provides you with beautiful outlooks of Mount Rainier, the Nisqually Valley, and the Tatoosh Range. This road is only open in the summer months.

If you want to go outside while staying in the park and are up for some hiking, there are plenty of options within the Longmire area. Enough to keep you busy for a few days.

Definitely don't miss taking the Historic District Walking Tour. This is a self-guided 60-minute tour that introduces you to all the historic buildings in the district.

If you want to start off slow, take the Twin Firs Trail. This short 0.4-mile trail starts two miles west of Longmire and is a short loop that takes you through old-growth forest.

Then you can move up to the 0.7-mile Trail of the Shadows. This is an easy walk past the earliest homestead in the park, the Longmire hot springs, and the forests around it.

The Carter Falls Trail is a 2-mile hike which begins 0.1 miles below the Cougar Rock Campgrounds. It is an easy walk among old-growth forest along the Paradise River. Once you pass Carter Falls, continue for 150 feet to view Madcap Falls.

Rampart Ridge Trail branches off from the Trail of the Shadows and is a steep loop trail of 4.6 miles. From here, you can enjoy the breathtaking sight of Mount Rainier and Nisqually Valley.

The Eagle Peak Trail is another steep trail that takes you through old-growth forest with views of Mount Rainier, Nisqually Valley, and the Tatoosh Range. The trailhead is found across the bridge at Longmire on the east side of the Nisqually River.

Lastly, there is the Narada Falls Trail. This 9-mile hike follows the Nisqually River via the Wonderland Trail from Longmire. This is a forest trail that takes you past Carter and Madcap Falls.

OLYMPIC NATIONAL PARK

The second leg of your trip will take you to Olympic National Park. This park has 611 miles of trails that many visitors don't get to experience because there simply isn't enough time on a short trip. We'll consider this in depth in a little bit. For now, let's talk about how you can highlight all the park has to offer in a short trip of a few days.

The most traveled hikes are those in the north and western sides of the park. Start your trip by taking a hike through the Hoh Rainforest on either the Hall of Mosses Trail or the Hoh River Trail. Either of these will allow you to view iconic rainforest scenes. You'll see old growth timber, cathedrals of moss and ferns, and possibly some elk. Once you've spent the day in the rainforest, get a good night's rest so you can explore the coastal area next.

The coastal area is about an hour drive from the Hoh Rainforest. Begin your day at the beaches of La Push. There will be miles of beach-hiking to enjoy that includes sea stacks and tide pools.

The two must-sees here are Rialto Beach and Hole in the Wall. A little farther south you can visit Second Beach which is a little less crowded if you want some solitude. Stay at this beach to enjoy the sunset before heading back to your campsite for the night.

The next day, consider visiting the Lake Crescent region on the northern flank of the park. Here you can find hiking trails that give you access to waterfalls and mountains. Not to be missed is the Spruce Railroad Trail that has a wonderful bridge over the Devil's Punchbowl. If you want to see waterfalls, then remember to visit the short trail that takes you to Sol Duc Falls just a few miles away from Sol Duc Hot Springs.

If you still have time after seeing the rivers, lakes, rainforests, and the coast of Olympic National Park, go on a hike up Hurricane Ridge. This will give you remarkable vistas of the ridge lines in the park. Two wonderful hikes to take if you have a moment to spare are the Hurricane Hill and the Klahhane Ridge. In the summer you can hike the area and view wildflowers, marmots, and mountain goats. When you are ready, head to the last stop of your trip.

NORTH CASCADES

End your trip in the North Cascades National Park. If you are going to stay a few nights here, your best option is Stehekin Valley. This is a way to truly get away from the hustle of the modern world and enjoy nature. The valley is located at the headwaters of Lake Chelan, the third deepest lake in the United States.

Part of the experience is getting to Stehekin since it is connected to the outside world only by foot, boat, or plane. Once you arrive, you will find a range of historical, cultural, and outdoor activities that will connect you with your surroundings. Stehekin places you at the crossroads of the Lake Chelan Recreation Area and the North Cascades National Park Complex.

You can camp here in a variety of settings based on what you prefer: lakeside, roadside, or backpacking. Most sites are small and primitive, with the exception of the lakeside sites. All require a backcountry permit that you can get from the visitor center.

While lakeside sites don't need a backcountry permit, private boaters will need a Federal Dock permit. There is also a lodge in the area if you prefer to stay in an indoor, more modern sort of environment.

While staying in this destination, there are a number of hikes you can enjoy no matter what your preference and ability might be:

Agnes Gorge is a 2.5-mile route that is perfect for a day hike. It offers lovely vistas of Agnes Mountain and ends at the deep Agnes Gorge, which has a beautiful fresh waterfall in the spring. Along the way, you can enjoy the variety of plant communities.

The Imus Creek Loop is only 0.8 miles. It is a self-guided nature trail that has you walk near the astounding Lake Chelan and the lower Stehekin Valley.

Lakeshore is a longer 17.2-mile hike that follows the scenic north shore of Lake Chelan. This is a great option for early morning or evening hikes. At the mile mark, you will enjoy panoramic views of McGregor Mountain.

At 3.5 miles, you can view Flick Creek and Moore Point at 7 miles– both of which are favorable day-hike destinations. There are private homes along this trail, so proceed with caution when it comes to loud disruptive noises for larger hiking parties, or accidentally walking through someone's property without permission.

Buckner Orchard Loop is a variable length trail. In contrast, Buckner Lane is a short forest walk that follows an old irrigation ditch that still provides life to the orchard. A self-guided tour booklet at two locations in the orchard give you the story of the Buckner Family.

The Historical Buckner Orchard is a National Historic Place that was a commercial orchard until the 1920s. It is one of the best preserved historic orchards in the United States today and still produces the "Common Delicious" apples.

The Stehekin River hike is a 4-mile trail that starts at the Stehekin airstrip and follows the river to Weaver Point. Along with this trail, you can enjoy spring flowers, beaver ponds, woodpeckers, and kokanee salmon in the fall months. This trail is shaded and relatively leveled– the makings for an easy hike.

The Old Wagon Trail is a 5.2-mile route part of the Pacific Crest Trail. It takes you north to State Route 20, then eventually to Manning Provincial Park in Canada.

MODERATE HIKES

Agnes Creek is a 5.5-mile hike as a part of the southbound Pacific Crest Trail. The entire trail ends at the border of Mexico, but it is also an excellent day hike along the Agnes River. Along the way, you can enjoy a forested hike of large western red cedars.

Howard Lake is a short 1.3-mile hike that offers lots of opportunities for bird watching. You'll also get to enjoy views of Agnes Mountain to the southwest. You can increase the hike to a loop if you look for the turn out one mile past Howard Lake to take you back to Stehekin Valley Road.

Rainbow Loop is a 4.4-mile hike that leads you to open bluffs overlooking the scenic Stehekin River Valley and the historic Buckner Orchard. Take a stop at the bridge over Rainbow Creek at the 2.5-mile mark.

STRENUOUS HIKES

McGregor Mountain is a 7.7-mile hike toward the summit of the mountain. From here, you can have a moment to yourself in order to capture memorable images of both the Stehekin and Agnes drainages. The last half mile of this hike is a hand and foot scramble up talus and ledges to reach the summit. Be sure to check for snow conditions before attempting this hike.

Purple Creek is a 7.5-mile road that features 57 switchbacks that lead to a rewarding view of the valley and Lake Chelan. If you're up for an additional half-mile hike to Boulder Butter, you can discover 360-degree views of Lake Juanita. This hike is hot in the summer and has no water for two miles, so one is at a great risk for dehydration if they are not properly prepared.

PART – 4

A DETAIL IN-DEPTH LOOK INSIDE 3 MOST POPULAR PARKS

YOSEMITE, OLYMPIC & GRAND CANYON

IN-DEPTH GUIDE TO YOSEMITE NATIONAL PARK

Yosemite National Park is possibly one of the most popular and most visited National Parks in the United States. You could spend days in this park and still only see the highlight.

Depending on what your interests are, you should plan an in-depth visit to Yosemite. Let's take a close look at what activities and hikes you can do in each section of the park to help you plan how many days you should spend to see and do all you want.

YOSEMITE VALLEY

Yosemite Valley is the area where most tourists go. It is full of famous cliffs and waterfalls that have made Yosemite a popular destination for nature photographers and hikers alike. Most of the areas of Yosemite Valley are available year-round. Let's take a look at a few.

VISITOR CENTERS AND MUSEUMS

The Valley Visitor Center is open all year. Here you'll find an information desk, a bookstore, films, and exhibits on the park's geology, history, plant growth, and animal life.

The Valley Wilderness Center is open from May to October. Here you can get wilderness permits, bear canisters, maps, and guidebooks. This center can also give you information on pre-trip planning, instructions on minimum-impact camping, and the Yosemite Wilderness in general.

The Yosemite Museum is open all year. It includes the Indian Cultural Exhibit and Village that provides a look at the cultural history of the native Miwok and Paiute people who occupied the region from 1850. There are often demonstrations of skills the tribes used, such as weaving. A gallery also has periodic art exhibits throughout the year.

The Happy Isles Art and Nature Center is open from May to September. It is focused on families that want to explore nature by providing natural history exhibits, interactive displays, and art workshops. Nearby, it offers short trails that take you through the forest, rivers, and fern environments.

The Yosemite Conservation Heritage Center– once known as the LeConte Memorial Lodge– is open from late May to early September. This was the first public visitor center in Yosemite and was started by the Sierra Club. Today, it offers a children's corner, library, and programs on environmental education; a few of these programs are offered in the evening.

ACTIVITIES

- ☐ Art and Photography - All Year
- ☐ Biking - Spring to Fall
- ☐ Birdwatching - All Year
- ☐ Fishing - Spring to Fall
- ☐ Hiking and Walking - All Year
- ☐ Horseback Riding - Spring to Fall
- ☐ Ice Skating - Winter
- ☐ Ranger and Interpretive Programs - All Year
- ☐ Stargazing - All Year
- ☐ Guided Tours - All Year
- ☐ Watersports - Summer
- ☐ Camping - All Year

HIKING TRAILS

Trail	Difficulty	Length
Bridalveil Fall Trail	Easy	0.5-mile round trip
Lower Yosemite Fall Trail	Easy	1-mile loop
Cook's Meadow Loop	Easy	1-mile loop
Mirror Lake Loop	Easy/Moderate	2-mile lake & back 5-mile loop
Valley Loop Trail	Moderate	13-mile loop
Vernal Fall and Nevada Fall Trails	Moderate/Strenuous	1.6-8 mile round-trip
Yosemite Falls Trail	Moderate/Strenuous	2-7.2 mile round-trip
Snow Creek Trail	Strenuous	9.4-mile round-trip
Four Mile Trail	Strenuous	4.8 mile one way
Half Dome Trail	Strenuous	14-16.4 mile round-trip

POINTS OF INTEREST

WATERFALLS

Yosemite Valley features some of the most famous waterfalls in the park. The best time to see the waterfalls is in spring when runoff is at its peak. In the summer and fall, the waterfalls have little to no water.

Yosemite Falls - 2,425 feet, flows November through July with a peak in May. This is one of the tallest waterfalls in the world and is actually comprised of three separate waterfalls: Upper Yosemite Fall standing at 1,430 feet, the Middle Cascades at 675 feet and Lower Yosemite Fall at 320 feet. There are several places in Yosemite Valley where you can see this waterfall– the best is around Yosemite Village and Yosemite Valley Lodge.

Sentinel Falls - 2,000 feet, flows March through June with a peak in May. This waterfall is found on the south side of Yosemite Valley near Sentinel Rock. It is another waterfall comprised of multiple cascades that range from 50 to 500 feet. The best places to see Sentinel Falls are found in Southside Drive near the Sentinel Beach Picnic Area and the Four Mile Trailhead. It is also possible to see it from Leidig Meadow or along the Upper Yosemite Fall Trail.

Ribbon Falls - 1,612 feet, flows March through June with a peak in May. This is the waterfall you typically see when driving into Yosemite Valley just after the turn for Bridalveil Fall.

Horsetail Falls - 1,000 feet, flows December through April. This particular waterfall is famous for appearing to be on fire when it reflects the sunset's bright orange glow in mid to late February. It is best seen from east of El Capitan.

Bridalveil Falls - 620 feet, flows all year with peak flow in May. This is typically the first waterfall people see when they enter the Yosemite Valley. It is best seen from the tunnels on the Wawona Road.

Nevada Falls - 594 feet, flows all year with peak flow in May. You can view Nevada Fall from a distance at Glacier Point.

Vernal Falls - 317 feet, flows all year with peak flow in May. Again, you can spot this from a distance at Glacier Point.

Illilouette Falls - 370 feet, flows all year with peak flow in May. You can catch it while hiking the trail to Vernal Fall, but the best viewing is on the Panorama Trail, a short way from Glacier Point. This waterfall isn't visible from roads, but rather only from steep hiking trails.

Tunnel View

Here you can discover one of the most famous views of the Yosemite Valley. It is found at the east end of the Wawona Tunnel along Wawona Road or Highway 41. You will be able to see El Capitan and Bridalveil Fall rising from the valley floor with Half Dome in the background.

El Capitan Meadow

When you visit this meadow, you'll be able to see straight up El Capitan while also viewing Cathedral Rocks. The meadow is located along the one-way Northside Drive, and it is best to stop on your route outside of the Yosemite Valley.

Valley View

Another stop along the one-way Northside Drive that you can visit on your way out of the valley is the Valley View vista. Here, you can view the valley while standing alongside the Merced River. It is located between the vista for Bridalveil Fall and Pohono Bridge. Look for it as you start to see directional signs for highways while leaving the park.

Sentinel Bridge

The Sentinel Bridge in the Yosemite Valley is famous for the view of Half Dome clearly reflected in the Merced River. You'll also be able to enjoy excellent panoramic views of Yosemite Falls.

WAWONA AND MARIPOSA GROVE

The Wawona basin was added to Yosemite National Park in 1932. The Mariposa Grove is the largest grove of sequoias in Yosemite, nearly 500 trees.

VISITOR CENTERS AND MUSEUMS

The Wawona Visitor Center is open from May to October. You'll find an information desk, exhibits, and galleries of paintings. You can also obtain wilderness permits here all throughout the year.

The Pioneer Yosemite History Center is open all 365 days of the year. You can visit historic buildings from the past. Exploration and demonstrations are available in the summer months.

ACTIVITIES

- ☐ Art and Photography - All Year
- ☐ Backpacking - All Year
- ☐ Birdwatching - All Year
- ☐ Camping - All Year
- ☐ Fishing - Spring to Fall
- ☐ Golfing - Spring to Fall
- ☐ Hiking and Walking - All Year
- ☐ Horseback Riding - Spring to Fall
- ☐ Picnicking - All Year
- ☐ Ranger and Interpretive Programs - All Year
- ☐ Watersports – Summer

HIKING TRAILS

Trail	Difficulty	Length
Wawona Meadow Loop	Easy	3.5-mile loop
Swinging Bridge Loop	Easy	4.8-mile loop
Big Trees Loop	Easy	0.3-mile loop
Grizzly Giant Loop Trail	Moderate	2-mile loop
Alder Creek	Strenuous	12 miles
Chilnualna Falls	Strenuous	8.2-mile round-trip
Guardians Loop Trail	Strenuous	6.5-mile round-trip
Mariposa Grove Trail	Strenuous	7-mile round-trip

POINTS OF INTEREST

CHILNUALNA FALLS

This waterfall flows all year and peaks in May. It is made up of five large cascades that flow through granite formations above the Wawona area. If you climb to the top, you'll be able to look out over the entire Wawona surroundings.

MARIPOSA GROVE

The entire Mariposa Grove of over 500 mature sequoias is a must-see.

TUOLUMNE MEADOWS AND TIOGA ROAD

This area is a large, open sub-alpine meadow that includes the winding Tuolumne River. The territory around the meadow is built up from domes and peaks. Tioga Road is a 47-mile scenic drive through the location that takes you from Crane Flat to Tioga Pass while going through forests, meadows, lakes, and granite domes. There are many turnouts with beautiful vistas to enjoy. Tioga Road is often open from late May or June until October or November.

VISITOR CENTERS AND MUSEUMS

The Tuolumne Meadows Visitor Center is open from about late May to late September. Here you'll find an information desk, bookstore, and exhibits on the geology, history, and both the plant and animal life in the area.

The Tuolumne Meadows Wilderness Center is open from about late May to October 14th. Here you can get wilderness permits, bear canisters, maps, and guidebooks. You can also get information on trip planning, minimum-impact camping, and the Yosemite Wilderness.

The Parsons Memorial Lodge is open from late June to early September. You can learn about the natural and human history of the meadows by taking a hike to the area where John Muir and Robert Underwood Johnson first thought of establishing the national park. The lodge is about a mile walk from the Lembert Dome parking lot or the Tuolumne Meadows Visitor Center.

ACTIVITIES

- ☐ Art and Photography - Summer and Fall
- ☐ Auto Touring - Summer and Fall
- ☐ Backpacking - All Year
- ☐ Birdwatching - Summer and Fall
- ☐ Camping - Summer
- ☐ Fishing - Summer and Fall
- ☐ Hiking and Walking - Summer and Fall
- ☐ Picnicking - Summer and Fall

☐ Ranger and Interpretive Programs - Summer

☐ Stargazing - Summer and Fall

☐ Horseback Riding - Summer

☐ Guided Tours - Summer

☐ Watersports - Summer

HIKING TRAILS

Trail	Difficulty	Length
Soda Springs and Parsons Lodge	Easy	1.5-mile round-trip
Lyell Canyon via John Muir Trail	Easy	8-mile round-trip
Elizabeth Lake	Moderate	4.8-mile round-trip
Gaylor Lakes	Moderate	2-mile round-trip
Cathedral Lakes	Moderate	7-mile round-trip
Mono Pass	Moderate	8-mile round-trip
Glen Aulin	Moderate	11-mile round-trip
Dog Lake and Lembert Dome	Moderate	2.8-4 mile round-trip
Vogelsang High Sierra Camp	Strenuous	13.8-mile round-trip

POINTS OF INTEREST

Siesta Lake

This alpine lake is found along the south portion of Tioga Road, about 13 miles east of the Crane Flat Gas Station. Swimming and picnicking in this area is popular.

White Wolf

This campground and concession area just north of Yosemite Valley along Tioga Road is a great place to use as a base for the majority of the surrounding hiking trails.

Yosemite Creek Picnic Area

Either before or after you leave Tuolumne Meadows, you should stop to enjoy lunch here. This lunch spot has beautiful scenery and is located right beside the creek. The area has picnic tables, vault toilets, garbage, and recycling services but no grills or water.

Olmsted Point

The location along Tioga Road– it looks down on the Yosemite Valley from the east. One of the more predominant peaks you'll see from here is Half Dome.

Tenaya Lake

A great area for picnicking, swimming, paddle boarding, kayaking, and canoeing. There are two picnic areas, out of which only one is wheelchair-accessible.

Soda Spring

Within a historic log cabin enclosure, you'll see a natural fountain of carbonated, cold water bubbling from the ground. The spring is located near the Parsons Lodge and can be reached by a short walk from the Lembert Dome parking area.

Tuolumne Meadows

The namesake of this area is one of the largest high-elevation meadows in the Sierra Nevada mountain range. At 8,600 feet, this meadow offers scenic views as well as a number of concession options.

Lembert Dome

Just north of the Tioga Road near the Tuolumne Meadows is this peak. Climb to the top to get excellent views of the meadows and the surrounding mountain peaks.

HETCH HETCHY

This area is peacefully located in the northwest corner of the park and is beautiful no matter what season you travel in. At 3,900 feet, Hetch Hetchy Valley has one of the longest hiking seasons in the park and is also a great place to see waterfalls and wildflowers.

In the summer months, the temperatures do rise, but not enough to ruin the reward of seeing the vast wilderness.

ACTIVITIES

- ☐ Backpacking - Spring to Fall
- ☐ Birdwatching - All Year
- ☐ Fishing - All Year
- ☐ Hiking - Spring to Fall
- ☐ Horseback Riding - Spring to Fall

HIKING TRAILS

Trail	Difficulty	Length
Lookout Point	Moderate	2-mile round-trip
Wapama Falls	Moderate	5-mile round-trip
Rancheria Falls	Moderate	13.4-mile round-trip

Smith Peak	Moderate to Strenuous	13.5-mile round-trip
Poopenaut Valley	Strenuous	3-mile round-trip

POINTS OF INTEREST

O'Shaughnessy Dam

Completed in 1938, this dam now serves as a 117-billion gallon reservoir for the Bay Area. Downstream, two hydroelectric plants provide power.

Wapama Fall

You can reach this scenic wonder via a trail that follows the shoreline of the reservoir. At the top, you can overlook Tueeulala and Wapama Falls.

Smith Peak

At 7,751 feet, this is the highest point in the park and provides breathtaking sights. There are two trailhead options that can take you to the top of this mountain.

Poopenaut Trail

Starts about four miles past the entrance station. It is a short but strenuous hike that leads you to the Tuolumne River.

CRANE FLAT AREA

A part of Yosemite that features pleasant forests and meadows full of wildflowers depending on the season in case. The Tuolumne and Merced Groves of sequoias are nearby and only accessible by foot.

ACTIVITIES

- ☐ Birdwatching - All Year
- ☐ Camping - Summer
- ☐ Hiking and Walking - Spring to Fall
- ☐ Winter Sports - Winter

HIKING TRAILS

Trail	Difficulty	Length
Lukens Lake from Tioga Road	Easy	1.6-mile round-trip
Tuolumne Grove and Nature Trail	Moderate	2.5-mile round-trip
Merced Grove	Moderate	3-mile round-trip
Lukens Lake from White Wolf	Moderate	4.6-mile round-trip
Harden Lake	Moderate	5.8-mile round -trip
May Lake	Moderate	2.4-mile round-trip
North Dome	Strenuous	10.4-mile round-trip
Ten Lakes	Strenuous	12.6-mile round-trip

POINTS OF INTEREST

Merced Grove of Giant Sequoias

Located on Big Oak Flat Road west of Crane Flat, this grove features about two dozen sequoias. Parking is limited, and there is no water, so come prepared.

Tuolumne Grove of Giant Sequoias

Located along Tioga Road east of Crane Flat, this grove features about two dozen sequoias. Once again, there is limited parking and no services that provide clean water, so you'll need to come prepared.

Crane Flat Snow Play Area

This can be a great place to go in the winter to enjoy sledding. It is located south of the Crane Flat Gas Station near the campground. The area is open when there is sufficient snow.

IN-DEPTH GUIDE TO OLYMPIC NATIONAL PARK

The Olympic National Park is a very diverse park with a lot of areas to see. There are all kinds of biomes, from temperate rainforests and old growth forests to a wild coast with sandy beaches and rugged, glacier-capped mountains. With so much wilderness to explore, you can easily spend a week or more here.

Let's look at each area of the park and the recreational opportunities they provide. This can help you plan for which sections of the park you want to visit and how many days you'll likely need to spend there.

PACIFIC COAST

The coastal areas of Olympic National Park provide you with diverse landscapes varying from sea stacks and crystal waters, to old growth forests. Let's consider the three main areas of the Pacific Coast in the park.

KALALOCH AND RUBY BEACH

LOCATION

Kalaloch is one of the most visited areas of Olympic National Park. Kalaloch and Ruby Beach are located directly off Highway 101 on the Olympic Peninsula, on the southwest coast. These coastal waters provide a safe haven for thousands of marine species. Three national wildlife refuges and the Olympic Coast National Marine Sanctuary protect these waters.

RECREATION

The Olympic Peninsula features some amazingly pristine beaches and an abundance of marine wildlife as well. North of Ruby Beach there is the natural boundary of the Hoh River. There are three hiking trails that allow you to enjoy the beautiful natural sights of this area:

1. Beach 4: 0.2 miles, one-way.
2. Ruby Beach: 0.2 miles, one-way.
3. Kalaloch Nature Trail: 0.8-mile loop.

This is also a great location for bird-watching. Common birds spotted in the area are western gulls, bald eagles, and other coastal birds.

Beach 4 is a great place to go for tidepooling. Here you'll see sea stars and anemones in various colors and sizes. Make sure you check the current tide charts before hiking along the coast. During high tides, some areas may be impassable, and you'll need to use overland trails.

WHERE TO STAY

Kalaloch and South Beach are the only campgrounds on the southern coast of Olympic National Park. Kalaloch is open year round with 175 sites, four of which offer wheelchair access. You should make your reservations as early in the year as possible. South Beach is just to the south and has 50 sites, but is only open from Memorial Day to late September.

Another option is Kalaloch Lodge, located right on the beach. With reservations, you can get a room or cabin.

MORA AND RIALTO BEACH

LOCATION

Rialto Beach is defined by rocky beaches, giant drift logs, and offshore islands known as sea stacks. Just inland is the Mora area characterized by towering trees with lush undergrowth.

Rialto Beach is about 36 miles southwest of Lake Crescent and about 75 miles from Port Angeles. You can get to via Mora Road off La Push Road.

RECREATION

About 1.5 miles north of Rialto Beach within the Olympic wilderness you can view the sea-carved arch known as Hole-in-the-Wall. Always make sure you check the tide charts before hiking the coast to makes sure you avoid areas that are impassable.

There are seven hiking trails to consider in this section:

1. James Pond Trail: 0.3-mile loop.
2. Slough Trail: 0.9 miles.
3. Rialto Beach: 200 feet.
4. North Coast: 20.6 miles.
5. Second Beach: 0.7 miles.
6. Third Beach: 1.4 miles.
7. South Coast: 17.1 miles.

WHERE TO STAY

Three miles from Rialto Beach is the Mora Campground with 94 sites. You can also choose to stay in the nearby town of Forks.

OZETTE

LOCATION

Lake Ozette presents a very diverse landscape: crystal clear lake waters, sea stacks off the coast, and old growth forests. It is located on the northwestern coast of the Olympic Peninsula and is reached via Hoko-Ozette Road off Highway 112.

RECREATION

You can visit the Makah Cultural and Research Center in Neah Bay if you want to learn about the rich history of the park. There is a 300 year-old preserved village that has been recovered here with over 50,000 artifacts from cultures dating back to 2,000 years.

There are three gorgeous hiking trails that allow you to explore the area. Just make sure you check tide charts to make sure there are no impassable spots:

1. Cape Alava: 3.1 miles.
2. Sandpoint: 2.8 miles, one-way.
3. Ozette Loop: 3.1 miles.

WHERE TO STAY

A 15-site campground sits beside Lake Ozette and offers excellent views. Just outside the park at Ozette, you can rent cabins and campsites. You can also choose to stay at the nearby towns of Clallam Bay and Sekiu.

TEMPERATE RAINFORESTS

Just west of the Olympic Mountains you'll find temperate rainforests where the annual rainfall is about 12 to 14 feet. Here you can walk among a lush green canopy of deciduous and coniferous trees while the undergrowth is a thick bed of moss and ferns. Let's look at the two main areas that feature temperate rainforests.

HOH RAINFOREST

LOCATION

The Hoh Rainforest is one of the best remaining examples of temperate rainforest in the United States and is one of the top visitor destinations in the Olympic National Park. It is located on the west side of the Olympic National Park and is accessed from the Upper Hoh Road off Highway 101 about an hour from Forks and two hours from Port Angeles.

RECREATION

At the end of Upper Hoh Road, you should start your visit at the Hoh Rainforest Visitor Center. Here you can view exhibits about the area and get information about what to see and do on your visit. The center is open daily during the summer and closed December to early March. It is often open Friday through Sunday in the spring and fall.

To explore the beauty of the zone, there are two short nature loops near the Visitor Center:

1. The Hall of Mosses Trail: 0.8 miles.
2. The Spruce Nature Trail: 1.2 miles.

The major hiking trail in this particular location is the Hoh River Trail at 17.3 miles. It takes you to Glacier Meadow on the side of Mount Olympus. A branch off from this trail is the Hoh Lake Trail that guides you to Bogachiel Peak located between the Hoh Rainforest and the Sol Duc Valley.

WHERE TO STAY

There is a campground with 88 sites that is open year-round in the Hoh Rainforest. It is located among old growth forest along the river. You can also choose to stay in the nearby town of Forks which is less than an hour drive away by car.

QUINAULT RAINFOREST

LOCATION

The Quinault Rainforest is an ideal wilderness getaway. Not only do you get to enjoy a lush rainforest, but it is surrounded by alpine meadows, lakes and ice-carved mountain peaks. It is located at the southwestern area of the park and is about an hour from Forks and three hours from Port Angeles. It has a number of scenic drives and short loop hikes to keep you busy enjoying all the natural beauty around you.

RECREATION

The main activity here is hiking. There are four wonderful hikes to consider that allow you to see everything this section of the park has to offer:

1. Maple Glade: 0.5-mile loop.
2. Kestner Homestead: 1.3-mile loop.
3. Cascading Terraces: 0.5-mile trail.
4. Irely Lake: 1.1-mile trail.

WHERE TO STAY

There are two campground options in the Quinault Rainforest. The North Fork Campground has 9 sites, and the Graves Creek Campground has 30 sites. You can also choose lodging options in the surrounding sections.

ELWHA VALLEY

LOCATION

Along the Olympic Peninsula, the Elwha Valley is the largest watershed, and in the early 1900s was known for its salmon population. It is located in the central northern region of the park about 11 miles west of Port Angeles. You can reach it via the Olympic Hot Springs Road off Highway 101.

RECREATION

There are plenty of sightseeing options from your vehicle along Olympic Hot Springs Road and Whiskey Bend Road if you want to take an auto tour.

You can also fish, but keep in mind it is catch and release only.

Lastly, there are several hiking options to keep you busy and allow you to see the true wonders of this region.

1. Madison Falls: 0.1 miles, one-way trail.
2. Cascade Rock: 2.1 miles, one-way trail.
3. Griff Creek: 2.8 miles, one-way trail.
4. West Elwha: 3.2 miles, one-way trail.
5. Humes Ranch Loop: 6.5-mile loop.
6. Elwha-Hurricane Hill: 6.2 miles, one-way trail.
7. Wolf Creek: 7.9 miles, one-way trail.
8. Smokey Bottom: 1.9 miles, one-way trail.
9. Smokey Hill: 0.5 miles, one-way trail.
10. Boulder Lake: 5.9 miles, one-way trail.
11. Olympic Hot Springs / Appleton Pass: 7.7 miles, one-way trail.

WHERE TO STAY

There are no campgrounds in the valley area, but you can stay at other campgrounds in the park or at lodging in nearby towns.

LAKE CRESCENT

LOCATION

This lake is located at the foothills to the Olympic Mountains about 18 miles west of Port Angeles. There is a natural beauty to this lake with plenty of recreational options.

RECREATION

There are a lot of picnic options that provide a beautiful and quiet scene for lunch:

1. Fairholme
2. Bovee's Meadow
3. La Poel
4. The North Shore

In the summer and fall, this is a great option for those looking to get out on the water. Both east and west ends of the lake feature boat launches. You can rent rowboats from the Lake Crescent Lodge. Kayaking and sailing are two popular water activities here.

There are also a number of hiking trails that allow you to take in the natural beauty:

1. Marymere Falls: 0.9 miles, one-way trail.
2. Moments in Time: 0.6-mile loop trail.

3. Mount Storm King: 2.2 miles, one-way trail.

4. Spruce Railroad: 4 miles, one-way trail.

5. Fairholme Campground Loop: 0.8-mile loop trail.

6. Pyramid Peak: 3.5 miles, one-way trail.

7. Aurora Creek: 3.4 miles, one-way trail.

8. Barnes Creek: 7.5 miles, one-way trail.

WHERE TO STAY

The Fairholme Campground with 87 sites is on the west end of the lake and has one wheelchair accessible site.

If you prefer not to stay at a campground, there is also Lake Crescent Lodge or the Log Cabin Resort. Both are open from late spring until early fall. Rooms and cottages are available for reservation.

SOL DUC VALLEY

LOCATION

The Sol Duc Valley is full of old growth forests, subalpine lakes, and snowy mountain peaks. The Sol Duc River is also filled with coho salmon. It is found in the northwest region of the park, about 40 minutes west of Port Angeles and is accessed via Sol Duc Road off Highway 101.

RECREATION

There are a number of hiking trails to enjoy in the Sol Duc Valley:

1. Sol Duc Falls: 0.8 miles, one-way trail.

2. Lover's Lane: 6.0-mile loop trail.

3. Ancient Groves: 0.6-mile loop trail.

4. Mink Lake: 2.6 miles, one-way trail.

5. Deer Lake: 3.8 miles, one-way trail.

After a long day on the trail, you can head over to the Sol Duc Hot Springs Resort where you'll find a range of activities including a mineral pools, massages, and dining options.

WHERE TO STAY

The Sol Duc Campground has 82 sites in old growth forest alongside the river. The Sol Duc Hot Springs Resort is also available for lodging as well as an RV campground. Campground sites are first come, first served– but you need to make reservations for the resort or RV campground.

The Resort is typically open from late March through the last weekend in October. You can also choose to stay in the nearby towns of Forks or Port Angeles.

HURRICANE RIDGE

LOCATION

Hurricane Ridge is the easiest mountainous area to access within the Olympic National Park. Throughout the year you can enjoy beautiful views due to clear weather. It is found about 17 miles south of Port Angeles via Hurricane Ridge Road off Mount Angeles Road.

RECREATION

A good place to start is the Hurricane Ridge Visitor Center. You'll find this just before the end of the road and inside you can get brochures, maps, snacks, and tips for your time in the area.

There are also numerous trails to enjoy:

1. Cirque Rim: 0.5 miles, one-way trail.

2. Big Meadow: 0.25 miles, one way trail.

3. High Ridge: 0.5-mile loop trail.

4. Klahhane Ridge: 3.8 miles, one-way trail.

5. Hurricane Hill: 1.6 miles, one-way trail.

6. Wolf Creek: 8.0 miles, one-way trail.

7. Little River: 8.0 miles, one-way trail.

8. Hurricane Hill/Elwha: 6.0 miles, one-way trail.

In the winter months, you can bask in the scenery along with the winter sports of snowshoeing, cross-country skiing, and sledding.

WHERE TO STAY

Heart O' the Hills is the nearest campground at 12 miles north of Hurricane Ridge and 5 miles south of Port Angeles. This campground features 105 sites in an old-growth forest. You can also lodge at the nearby town of Port Angeles.

DEER PARK

LOCATION

The Deer Park is an 18-mile road that is narrow and steep and not recommended for RVs or trailers. It is located about 9 miles from Highway 101.

RECREATION

There are four wonderful hikes to explore:
1. Rain Shadow Loop: 0.5-mile loop trail.

2. Deer Park to Obstruction Point: 7.4 miles, one-way trail.

3. Three Forks: 4.3 miles, one-way trail.

4. Deer Ridge: 4.6 miles, one-way trail.

WHERE TO STAY

There are 14 sites available in this area. Potable water isn't available, so plan accordingly.

STAIRCASE

LOCATION

The staircase is located on the southeastern side of the Olympic Peninsula. It is about an hour drive from Olympia and two hours south of Port Angeles. The access road is unpaved, so check road conditions before venturing there.

RECREATION

There are quite a few hiking trails that allow you to enjoy this beautiful area of the park:

1. Staircase Rapids Loop: 2 miles, one-way trail.
2. Four Stream: 1.2 miles, one-way trail.
3. Wagonwheel Lake: 2.9 miles, one-way trail.
4. Shady Lane: 0.9 miles, one-way trail.
5. Flapjack Lakes: 7.8 miles, one-way trail.
6. North Fork Skokomish River: 15.1 miles, one-way trail.

WHERE TO STAY

There is a campground that has 47 sites. Otherwise, you can lodge at any of the places in the nearby Mason County.

IN-DEPTH GUIDE TO GRAND CANYON NATIONAL PARK

The Grand Canyon is a place you have to see to really appreciate and enjoy. For many, it is a once in a lifetime opportunity to visit this majestic national park.

Whether you've never been to the Grand Canyon or you are returning, take the time to look through this in-depth guide on the four sections of the Grand Canyon and plan your trip to get the most out of it and see all this wonderful place has to offer.

SOUTH RIM

The main center of activity for people visiting the Grand Canyon is the South Rim. This part of the Grand Canyon is open year-round and offers lots of activities for all interests and outdoor activity levels. There are three main areas of interest you want to take the time to visit while at the Grand Canyon:

1. The Visitor Center / Mather Point is where you should head to get your first view of the Grand Canyon. This is also the main transit center if you want to get a free shuttle bus to further explore the South Rim.
2. The Market Plaza is the main business center of the South Rim with a general store, bank, and post office.
3. The Historic District is the village that started in the early pioneer days and houses the railroad depot and original lodges.

To get around the Grand Canyon village, you can take the Village Shuttle Bus. This connects you to the parking spots, the lodges, campgrounds, restaurants, and shops. The fastest way to get around the entire area and see the scenes is to take a ride on the Kaibab Rim Shuttle Bus. This bus provides you with the only access to the South Kaibab Trailhead and Yaki Point.

Another option is to take the Scenic Hermit Road Shuttle Route which operates from March 1st to November 30th. This bus stops at nine canyon overlooks along a scenic 7-mile road to the west of the village. The road is only open to private vehicles between December 1st and February 28th.

The place to start when visiting the Grand Canyon is the Grand Canyon Visitor Center. This is located just south of Mather Point. Here you'll find outdoor exhibits that provide you with information about the park and ideas for what to do while visiting. It is also recommended that you watch the film Grand Canyon: A Journey of Wonder while at the Visitor Center. The movie is about 20 minutes long and starts every one and a half hours.

From the Visitor Center, you can walk to the canyon rim and Mather Point by following pedestrian paths that take you to the Rim Trail.

Within the Grand Canyon Village, you'll find the Historic District. This is where the development of the South Rim started, and it was predominantly because of the Santa Fe Railroad in the early part of the 20th century. Several of the buildings here date back to the early 1900s including the popular Lookout Studio and Hope House.

Be sure to stop by the Train Depot and take one of the walking tours. Trains arrive at the Train Depot at least once a day.

While there also be sure to visit the Verkamp's Visitor Center. Here you can learn more about the history of the community.

Lastly, stop by the Kolb Studio where you will see art exhibits in the building that was once home to the early photographers of the region.

Visit Verkamp's Visitor Center, formerly a curio shop, to learn more about the history of this community. A Grand Canyon Association bookstore within this visitor center is a great place to browse for gifts.

Take a walk along the Greenway Trail. The segment of this trail starts across the street from the Train Depot and takes you from the Village to Market Plaza. It gives you a safe way to get around other than using the busy main roads.

At Market Plaza, you'll find the business center of the Grand Canyon Village. This is where you'll find services such as a general store, a bank, the post office, and a cafeteria. You can also choose to stay at the Yavapai Lodge.

During your stay, you should head one mile east to the Yavapai Museum of Geology. Here you can enjoy beautiful views of the Grand Canyon. You'll also be able to be entertained by geological displays with 3D models, photographs, and exhibits that discuss the geology of the area.

If you would rather get out and hike, then there are a couple of options along the South Rim of the Grand Canyon.

The Rim Trail follows the rim of the canyon for 13 miles. You can hike as much of this trail as you want and it can easily take all day to cover the entire trail. It is a fairly easy route for all levels of hikers.

The Bright Angel Trail is a steep road that takes you into the canyon and starts at the Bright Angel Lodge. It can be 3 to 9.2 miles depending on how far you want to hike. It can take up to nine hours to hike this trail.

DESERT VIEW

This small settlement is located about 25 miles east of the Grand Canyon Village in the South Rim area, along with the eastern edge of the Grand Canyon. A scenic road known as Desert View Drive connects the Grand Canyon Village to Desert View. If you are entering the park from the east, stopping at Desert View will give you your first glimpses of the Grand Canyon.

Desert View offers some excellent sights, but also offers other attractions as well. You can enjoy various park ranger programs and cultural demonstrations. Be sure to stop by the historic watchtower and Tusayan Museum.

Desert View has a visitor station in the watchtower and restrooms as well as a seasonal campground. There is a service station as well as a general store for your service needs. There are no additional lodging options at Desert View.

DESERT VIEW WATCHTOWER

This is an unusual stone tower that was designed in 1932 by architect Mary Colter. It is built in the style of ancient Puebloan towers. Climb the 85 steps to the observation deck– 70 feet up– to enjoy 360-degree views of the surrounding area. You are also able to take delight in wall murals that were created by the Hopi artist Fred Kabotie. Regular cultural demonstrations occur.

TUSAYAN RUIN AND MUSEUM

Here you can see the ruins of a small Ancestral Puebloan Village about 3 miles west of Desert View. This community produced pottery, arrowheads, and other household artifacts. There is a mostly flat 0.1-mile self-guided trail around the site, or you can take a ranger-led tour in the summer season that occurs at 11am and 2pm. At the museum, you can see exhibits that bring to life how Pueblo Indians lived.

NORTH RIM

The North Rim of the Grand Canyon has a short season and is only open from May 15th through October 15th. This is a good option for those who want to enjoy a less crowded touristic area of the Grand Canyon. Only about 10% of the visitors in the Grand Canyon head to the North Rim.

The North Rim is over 8,000 feet in elevation. There is one campground and the Grand Canyon Lodge available for lodging options. It is highly recommended to make reservations for both.

The North Rim is closed in the winter months due to snow.

Hiking across the canyon from the South Rim is about 21 miles. On the other hand, driving across takes five hours and is about 220 miles.

Your first stop at the North Rim should be the Visitor Center. It is next to the parking lot for the Grand Canyon Lodge and Bright Angel Point. Here you'll find park information, maps, brochures, and exhibits. The visitor center is open from May 15 to October 15.

During the open season, you can also find a range of interactive ranger programs offered from the visitor center. Behind the building, you'll also find numerous outdoor exhibits.

For the best views of the North Rim, start at the Grand Canyon Lodge patio and take the paved trail to the Bright Angel Point. This is a short and easy walk and gives you breathtaking views of Roaring Springs and Bright Angel Canyons.

Widforss Trail takes you along the rim for a total of 9.6 miles. It can take up to 6 hours to hike the full trail.

The North Kaibab Trail takes you down into the canyon. It can be up to 4 miles long depending on how far you choose to hike and can take up to 4 hours to hike the entire trail.

Go on a drive to enjoy the main peaks of this location. Point Imperial and Cape Royal offer short walks at the peak of each as well as many pull-outs along the way. It can easily take you a half day to complete all the stops and hikes while driving to these two scenic overlooks.

Point Imperial is the highest point on the North Rim at 8,803 feet and overlooks the Painted Desert as well as the eastern end of the Grand Canyon. Here you can also view the narrow walls of the Marble Canyon.

Cape Royal provides you with a panorama of the canyon with unlimited views to the east and west. It is a great spot to enjoy a sunrise or sunset. You can also bask in the glory of the Colorado River at Unkar Delta where it is framed by the Angels Window natural arch.

TUWEEP

For a true backcountry experience when visiting the Grand Canyon, consider heading to Tuweep. Here you have a very remote and rustic experience. Beware that access is challenging and will require you to negotiate difficult roadways. In the winter you have rain, snow, and freezing temperatures while the summer sees monsoonal rain and lightning. There are no services in this area. Before visiting, you need to know the following:

- [ ] You will need a high clearance vehicle.
- [ ] Road conditions can potentially change quickly.
- [ ] The day use area opens at sunrise to 30 minutes past sunset, and then the gate is locked.
- [ ] Camping requires a permit, and you need to arrive before sunset.
- [ ] The number of allowed vehicles is limited to four or less.
- [ ] All pets need to be leashed and restricted to the campground or open roads.
- [ ] Remember to remove and pack out all garbage.
- [ ] Come prepared since there is no water available.
- [ ] Vehicles longer than 22 feet are prohibited, this includes anything towed.
- [ ] All off-road vehicles must display highway license plates.
- [ ] Fires and charcoal grills are prohibited.
- [ ] No collecting or hunting is allowed.
- [ ] No drones or base jumping of any kind is allowed.

Staying at the campground in Tuweep allows you to experience sunsets, sunrises, and beautiful stargazing opportunities. You will need to get a permit to camp here. You can obtain a permit by going to www.nps.gov/grca/planyourvisit/backcountry-permit.htm.

You cannot get permits at the campground. There are only nine campsites for one to six people and a maximum of two vehicles. There is one large group campsite that holds seven to eleven people and up to four vehicles. The campsites have a seven-night limit, and stock animals aren't allowed.

While staying here, there are several things you need to experience.

TOROWEAP OVERLOOK

This viewpoint is dramatically different from others at the Grand Canyon. Here you look out over a gorge in a broad corridor 3,000 feet below the rim. The landscape is covered with ancient lava flows and black cinders cones.

You can even walk to the end if you want. To the west, you'll be able to see the largest rapid on the Colorado River.

TUWEEP HIKING TRAILS

There are two established hiking trails that you can access while in the area. The trailheads are signed, and you can find piles of rock that mark the path. Plan your hike in advance and make sure you keep in mind that there is no water and shade is scarce. There are no pets, bicycles, or vehicles allowed on the trails.

TUCKUP TRAIL

This trail allows you to view and experience Esplanade slick-rock along an old prospector's path. The three-mile trail will take you to Cove Canyon where you can enjoy an inner-canyon with beautiful views. The trailhead is north of Tuweep Campground.

SADDLE HORSE LOOP TRAIL

This is a 45-minute loop trail that provides you with beautiful views of the Colorado River. Along the way, you can walk among native plant gardens that are protected by ancient crusted soils.

The trail is accessed along the road between Toroweap Overlook and Tuweep Campground.

Just down the road from Tuweep, you can see this piece of history from the area. It is an antique pull grader from 1921 and the Toroweap Valley.

A FINAL NOTE

These are only a few of the many national parks scattered all throughout the United States, but they are incredibly worthwhile. They are natural landmarks for a reason, after all; it is not every day that one can find the largest living tree on Earth or a waterfall that looks as though it is flowing with liquid flaming gold. There is so much to see in this world, and these locations remind us of our insignificance compared to the powerful ground below us.

The earthy scent of falling rain, the crackle of gravel beneath our feet, the sensation of sunlight coating your skin. You cannot find that within the screen of a laptop or a phone.

Every now and then, it is a fundamental part of life to press a pause button on the world with day-to-day commodities and technology, and simply become one with nature, as we were once so many years ago. Being able to look top of a mountain at the world below you after hours of sweat and a burning feeling in your muscles during that last strenuous mile is one of the best, most unforgettable moments you will ever experience.

If hiking is not that much of a hobby or a way of life for you, simply taking a walk or photographing what you see in order to capture a single second of the sheer world of wonders in front of you is also more than enough.

Hopefully, this guide allowed you to brainstorm plans and future long-term trips to either of these national parks with friends, family, or even by your own accord as you search once again for the ultimate human connection to the planet we live in. Thank you, and best of luck in your adventures.

If you are interested in reading and learning about the all the National Parks in the Mountain regions, looks for my second book in this series.

Lastly, I want to say THANK YOU for purchasing and reading my book. I really hope you got a lot out of it!

Can I ask you for a quick favor though?

If you enjoyed this book, I would really appreciate it if you could leave me a Review.

I LOVE getting feedback from my wonderful readers, and reviews really do make the difference. I read all of my reviews and would love to hear your thoughts.

I also want to ask for your help and forgiveness ahead of time, in the event if you find any errors, typos or outdated information, please feel free to email me so I can fix the mistake.

bushcrafttrainer@gmail.com

Thank you so much!!

Rob J. Simms

Made in the USA
Middletown, DE
21 February 2019